THE ROAD
to
HOME RULE

Images of Scotland's Cause

CHRISTOPHER HARVIE
AND
PETER JONES

POLYGON

AT EDINBURGH

Polygon at Edinburgh
An imprint of Edinburgh University Press Ltd
22 George Square, Edinburgh

Typeset in Minion and Optima by
Pioneer Associates, Perthshire, and
printed and bound in Great Britain by
Redwood Books, Trowbridge, Wiltshire

A CIP Record for this book is available from the British Library

ISBN 1 902930 10 X (paperback)

The digital production of certain images of this publication was
supported through grant aid from the Scottish Cultural Resources
Access Network. Such assets are stored on the SCRAN ® system at
www.scran.ac.uk [Contact 0131 662 1211; *scran@scran.ac.uk*].
SCRAN is a registered trademark.

Contents

Preface

by Sir David Steel

© Scottish Parliament
Corporate Body 1999

Scottish History has certainly never moved in a linear fashion. External and internal influences have brought about complex and cataclysmic consequences that have resulted in the unique, if not peculiar, country that is Scotland. This critical but not unaffectionate account records some of the political, social and religious developments that have influenced Scotland's identity. This is a major contribution to the history of Scottish self-government.

Both wittingly and unwittingly the book illustrates the linkages Scotland has with the world outwith its borders. The book demonstrates the international character of the Scots. A country proud of its own heritage and culture, it has also contributed much in European and world affairs – just look at the Scottish Enlightenment. Today, the Scottish Parliament is also determined that we do not become insular in what we do but must engage with Westminster, Ireland, Wales, Europe, the Commonwealth and the rest of the World in every way it can.

While the writers of this book, with their considerable joint expertise, have differing views on the most effective way to govern Scotland, both see a continuing sense of consensus as valuable. The Scottish Parliament is facilitating that consensus in a Committee system that transcends party politics; ensuring effective scrutiny of government and others in a manner clearly more effective than that of the Westminster Parliament.

The Scottish Parliament was founded on accessibility and is determined to give people a more effective say in the democratic process – the Scots have a great appetite for debate and it is vital that every effort is made to stimulate and widen that debate. This book will help in that aim and will, I'm sure, generate widespread interest.

DAVID STEEL
Presiding Officer of the Scottish Parliament

Crossing the Border

For this is my country,
The land that begat me,
And these empty spaces
Are surely my own;
And the folk who toil here,
In the sweat of their faces,
Are flesh of my flesh
And bone of my bone.

Sir Alexander Gray, 'Scotland'

Scotland is a very odd kind of country. Drive up from England across the border, and you find plenty of evidence of a frontier of some sort – welcome signs and marker stones. The built landscape changes – from the red brick of northern England to the stone, high-pitched roofs and crow-stepped gables of traditional Scottish architecture. The change is not as ambiguous as in the marches of Wales where it would be difficult to see where Shropshire ends and Powys begins, but for the road signs which seem to double in size to accommodate bilingual Welsh and English names. Neither, when you reach your destination and turn on the television, can you find a dedicated Scottish TV channel as you can in Wales or the Basque Country of Spain. Sport apart, Scottish viewers watch much the same terrestrial television as is seen in every region of England, with the exception of chunks of different news and occasional current affairs programmes. And yet everyone seems to think that the Scots are very nationalistic, both fiercely proud and protective of Scottish culture and heritage and prone to shouting about independence. 'The end of a nightmare' was the melodramatic title that the Franco-German Arte channel gave to a documentary celebrating the new Scottish parliament.

If you are stopped by the police for a driving offence, however, you will find a big difference. You will be prosecuted by a procurator fiscal and may have to appear in a district or a sheriff court. This is not just a matter of different names, for Scotland has its own legal system, with its own codes of civil and criminal law. For those convicted of criminal offences, the highest court of appeal is a Scottish court, the Court of Session. And yet this legal system has survived for some 300 years without a legislature to keep updating it. Scotland has been the only country in the world with a legal system and no parliament. That, of course, has changed, and Scotland enters the new millennium with a parliament under construction opposite Holyrood Palace, ancient seat of the Scottish monarchs.

Now, to the visitor to Scotland this may look simple enough. A democratic nation has been without a parliament; democratic nations should have parliaments; therefore the Scots are getting what they should have had long ago. This is all perfectly logical and, after all, the kind of parliament or legislature that Canadian provinces, American states, German Länder, Australian states, Spanish regions and so on have all had for years, and yet few of them would claim to be a nation.

Scottish nationalism, which you would think – quite correctly – has been the engine behind the creation of this parliament, is deeply unstraightforward. Throughout the time it has been a feature of Scottish politics, it has taken on many forms – a romantic fashion, a non-sectarian movement, a with-us-or-against-us political party. It has had diverse goals and has adopted diverse stratagems: an incremental bit-by-bit approach or an all-or-nothing break-through dash. It has been quixotic – at times seeming an unstoppable inevitability and then just as quickly converting into a distant fantasy. For those who have wanted to be part of it, or just wanted to study it, it has, simultaneously, been exhilaratingly exciting and frustratingly mysterious.

One thing can be said about it with certainty. It takes two forms. One is Scottish Nationalism with a capital N, involving the payment of dues to a political party and loyalty to its cause. This has been part of politics in Scotland only since 1928. The other form is Scottish nationalism with a small n, a much longer tradition first detectable perhaps a thousand or so years ago in the resistance to the Viking invaders, elaborated in the late Middle Ages into something of a popular movement, in the proud words of the Declaration of Arbroath of 1320:

> for, as long as a hundred of us remain alive, we will never on any conditions be subjected to the lordship of the English. For we fight not for glory, or riches, or honour, but for freedom alone, which no good man gives up except with his life.

After a long lapse, this ideal of cultural identity and political freedom was revived, first in Victorian Scotland, and then with increasing emphasis in the twentieth century. It remains vigorously extant today.

These two forms are not necessarily mutually exclusive, though they would seem to be so at first sight. Small-n nationalists include people who would be horrified to be thought of as Nationalists. Such people might take out lawsuits if you described them as Nationalists and indeed fight the Scottish National

Party (SNP) at election time as though they are the party of the devil. Equally, Nationalists tend to regard none but their own as worthy of the name in any form. All non-Nationalists are Unionists and to a Nationalist this is not a term of simple classification, but an insult. Despite this apparently unbridgeable gulf, for a month or so in the autumn of 1997, Nationalists (the Scottish National Party) and Unionists (the Scottish Labour Party and the Scottish Liberal Democrats) managed to come together and successfully campaign for people to vote 'yes' to a Scottish parliament in a referendum, and 'yes' to that parliament having tax-raising powers. For that brief period, at least, they were all Scottish nationalists.

Evidently, the political definition of nationalism must encompass much more than just the straightforward goal of independence. Since 1945 and the effective end of the nineteenth-century concept of the independent state as an island ruggedly impervious to outside influence, independence has become a highly movable feast. There can no longer be one true definition of independence, only degrees of it; one politician's independence is another's subservience. In such a world, nationalism has to be defined as any political movement which seeks a gain, however small, of self-determination or control over a nation's own affairs.

And that, really, has been the story of Scottish nationalism: a long history of small gains, some due to the efforts of the Scots, some granted almost carelessly by others; some occurring by historical accident, some being wrested from an unwilling power by determined effort. At various times in their history, all political parties have espoused small-n nationalism of some sort. The Scottish parliament that we see now is another step in that long history.

There is another oddity about Scottish nationalism. It does not equate with any other nationalism to be found elsewhere in the world. Unlike Quebec or Flemish nationalism, there is no language motor. Fewer than 100,000 of the 5.1 million Scots speak Gaelic; many more can speak something of the Scots language (about which there is still debate as to whether it is a language or a dialect deriving from Northumbrian English), though few can write it. Independence would not mean bilingual or trilingual road signs.

Unlike the deeply unpleasant nationalisms of the Balkans, there is no ethnic element. The Scots are a mongrel nation of immigrants, from Ireland, Scandinavia, England, Italy, India, Pakistan and many other nations. Scottish nationalism is not based on anti-Englishness. True, there are occasional deplorable instances of English families who have been driven from their Scottish homes, but the SNP abhors such behaviour and does not engage in it, even covertly. Many national institutions, such as the National Galleries of Scotland, are run by English people yet no one campaigns for their removal. Indeed, one such director of the National Galleries, Timothy Clifford, ran into trouble when he proposed a new gallery devoted to Scottish art. He was vigor-ously opposed by Scots who felt that this was nothing but a cultural ghetto, depriving Scottish art of its international links and influences and removing it from the European cultural mainstream.

And unlike many other nationalisms, Scottish nationalism has no modern religious roots. Save for a brief and unsavoury period in the 1920s, when Protestants feared, and vainly tried to get the authorities to reverse, a tide of mainly Catholic Irish immigrants, there is no great religious divide in Scottish politics. Catholic and Protestant rivalries do exist, but these are local not national. Catholics, although they traditionally opposed independence as liable to lead to Protestant repression, are now perhaps more likely to vote for inde-pendence than Protestants. The head of the Roman Catholic Church in Scotland, Cardinal Tom Winning, is more prominent and perhaps more respected than the Moderator of the Church of Scotland, who changes annually. The man who has come to symbolise the country internationally, the actor Sean Connery, though a fervent SNP supporter, is of Irish Catholic and gypsy ancestry. The chief organiser of the Constitutional Convention which agreed on a scheme of home rule, Kenyon Wright, was a clergyman but an Episcopalian canon, though he symbolised a greater ecumenical tendency towards small-n nationalism as part of a 'global ethic'.

When the great English social historian Ralph Samuel died, he left instruc-tions that a piper was to play over his grave in Highgate Cemetery, a few yards from that of Karl Marx. As a wandering Jew, Samuel sympathised with a country which always argued about its identity, and the title of one of his books, *Theatres of Memory*, could almost sum up the Scots experience. 'This is a difficult country,' wrote Edwin Muir. 'Here things miscarry.' The drama can lurch from tragedy to farce. But at root it's serious, as Hugh MacDiarmid wrote to Dostoevsky:

Is Scotland big enough to be
A symbol of that force in me,
In wha's divine inebriety
A sicht abune contempt I'll see?
For a' that's Scottish is in me,
As a' things Russian were in thee,
And I in turn 'ud be an action
To pit in a concrete abstraction
My country's contrair qualities,
And mak' a unity o' these,
Till my love owre its history dwells,
As owretone to a peal o' bells.

'A Drunk Man looks at the Thistle'

In an age when identity can be either imaginatively civic, tapping and extending the ability of ordinary people, or murderously ethnic, the Scots, with their historical record and their world influence, have got to get things right.

CHAPTER ONE

Union to Sarajevo

What force or fraud could ne'er subdue
Thro' many warlike ages
Is wrought now by a coward few
For hireling traitor's wages
The English steel we could disdain,
Secure in valour's station;
But English gold has been our bane –
Such a parcel of rogues in a nation.

Robert Burns,
'A Parcel of Rogues in a Nation'

Let ilka ane roose the ford as they find it. I say, 'Let Glasgow flourish!'
Whilk is judiciously and elegantly putten round the town's armsd by way
of bye-word. Now, since St Mungo catch'd herrings in the Clyde, what was
ever like to gar us flourish like the sugar and tobacco trade? Will ony body
tell me that, and grumble at the treaty that opened us a road west-away
yonder?

Bailie Nicoll Jarvie, in Sir Walter Scott's *Rob Roy*, 1817

I

In history, you will be hard pressed to find a Scottish nationalism that fits any
kind of theory. The Union of 1707 – justifiably opposed by ordinary folk as
an aristocratic ramp – had itself elements of nationalism, in its preservation of
Calvinist religion, Scots law and education, in a period when famine and the
Darien disaster left the country weak. Even the great opponent of incorpo-
ration, Andrew Fletcher of Saltoun, wanted a federal union. The 'boasted
advantages' took time to turn up, but the Jacobite rebellions of 1715 and 1745
were less about Scottish independence than about the aim of James Francis
Edward Stewart, son of James VII, and Charles Edward Stewart, grandson of
the dethroned monarch: to regain the English throne. The slaughter of the
Highlanders at Culloden in 1746, which ended Jacobitism and suppressed the
Highlands, was cheerfully participated in by many Scots. The restoration of
tartan and bagpipes – the kitsch symbols of Scotland – was the masterstroke

of Sir Walter Scott, who choreographed the 1822 visit of George IV to Edinburgh and clad the monarch's retainers in abbreviated kilts. (The traditional Highland plaid covered the whole body.) A couple of industrious Englishmen, styling themselves the Sobieski-Stuarts, invented 'clan' tartans as society rushed to adopt the latest royal fashion.

Non-linguistic, non-ethnic, non-religious and carrying such symbolism, what is Scottish nationalism? This mystery and the intellectual challenge of unravelling it are perhaps why the characteristics of many *European* national movements can be traced back to Scottish precedents – even given the near-invisible place that Scotland occupies in world affairs. Yet in the intellectual world, Scotland has been a powerful presence. The Scottish Enlightenment, which lasted from 1730 to 1790, produced an extraordinary range of great thinkers: David Hume, moral philosopher; Adam Smith, political economist; James Hutton, founder of modern geology; Joseph Black, pioneering chemist; and many others. The peculiarity of this Scottish outpouring of the mind was the belief that advances, whether in philosophy or science, should have practical benefit, whether this was a better understanding of the morality of man or agricultural improvement. Thus the world flocked to Scotland to learn and it would have been astonishing in the nineteenth-century age of nationalist revolution if some lessons had not been drawn from Scotland.

G. M. Trevelyan, the English historian, wrote of William Wallace and Robert Bruce as precursors of popular nationalism. The German Romantic thinker Johann Gottfried Herder's identification of nation with language was derived from the impact made on him by James MacPherson's *Ossian*, an epic poem constructed (in part) from early Gaelic ballads and purporting to be written by the son of the mythical Celtic hero Fingal. Democratic poets like Germany's Friedrich Freiligrath and Hungary's Sandor Petofi consciously modelled themselves on Robert Burns with his paeans to the common man and woman. Historical novelists – Alessandro Manzoni in *The Betrothed*, Theodor Fontane in *Before the Storm* – were no less indebted to Walter Scott. But orthodox political nationalism, with its demands for constituent assemblies and national independence, and their links to plans for national development, was absent. As a result Scotland's national identity seemed to dwindle away. When Goethe wrote to his young Scots admirer, Thomas Carlyle, in the 1820s he noted the distinctiveness of Scotland. A century later the great Hungarian Marxist George Lukács, whose *Historical Novel* (1936) restored Scott's reputation, referred to him throughout as an 'English' novelist.

II

Yet this didn't in the least mean that the country lost its character. In 1945, when

Figure 1.1 James MacPherson, author of *Ossian*, 1761.
Unknown after Sir Joshua Reynolds. Provided by the Scottish National Portrait Gallery.
MacPherson's translations from the Gaelic of the ancient epic of *Ossian* caused a furore when published in 1761. They were scorned as forgeries by many contemporary English critics, and as enthusiastically taken up by Scottish literati. But in translation in Europe they were to be enthused over by such as Goethe and Herder and were to be crucial in creating the basis of many ethnic nationalist movements – uniting language, folk and nation, which were to blossom after the French Revolution.

Figure 1.2 The funeral of Sir Walter Scott at Dryburgh Abbey, 1832.
Print by Captain James Alexander, 1832. Provided by the Scottish National Portrait Gallery.
Scott's burial took place in a monument already dedicated to nationalism by the Earl of Buchan (1742–1829), antiquarian and controversialist, who erected a massive statue of William Wallace on the hillside above the abbey. Scott was a Tory and unionist but in his last years, with his polemics against the attempt to deprive Scotland of her rights of banknote issue, the 'Malagrowther letters', he emerged as a cultural nationalist.

the epoch of the European nation-state came to a messy end and one of your authors was wheeled in a pram to the by-election at which the SNP made its first, premature, breakthrough, Scotland was visibly quite distinct from its southern partner. Sir Alexander Gray, economist and poet, had captured this mixture of wildness and 'improvement' in 'Scotland' not many years earlier:

> Here in the uplands
> The soil is ungrateful;
> The fields, red with sorrel,
> Are stony and bare.
> A few trees, wind-twisted
> Or are they but bushes?

Stand stubbornly guarding
A home here or there.

Scooped out like a saucer,
The land lies before me;
The waters, once scattered,
Flow orderly now
Through fields where the ghosts
Of the marsh and the moorland
Still ride the old marches,
Despising the plough.

Emphasising difference became a way of coping with modernity. And Scots lived differently, huddled in cramped flats and steadings. They ate differently, and none too healthily. They worked disproportionately in the heavy industries and outdoors. Their worship and talk was near-incomprehensible to the English. Although the photos show people looking reasonably modern – the long-skirted, dark-suited formality of pre-1914 long past – the folk of 1945 were closer to the Victorians than to us. Television, plastics, contraception, mass motorisation, cheap foreign holidays, electronics: all of these were only to start making an impact in the 1960s.

But along with these innovations would come the sort of instability which made people look for new institutions. There were threats to existing jobs, forms of socialisation and personal relationships. The country became more violent than the squalid nineteenth century, when surprisingly few people were affected by crime. From being almost a subordinate order of creation, women became a central element of the labour force, though still badly rewarded. The sense of conviviality – largely male – in Scots society diminished. Less was done in clubs, churches, even in pubs; the 'bodies' of George Douglas Brown's 'Barbie' no longer conducted small-town politics in the main street. Yet the private sphere was no longer secure. In the twentieth century marriages would become no less frequent but less effective, over a third ending in divorce. Religious practice plummeted, although the belief in 'a force, not ourselves, making for righteousness' continued, in less orthodox forms.

This scale of change, though, was not new. Upheavals had been similarly intense during the first Industrial Revolution, when the main response throughout Europe had been for the masses to identify with the nation-state, as the institution competent enough to legislate for stability. In Scotland's case that state was Great Britain, although a range of 'Scottish' institutions – law, local government, education, religion – always remained, and these gave a tight direction to Scottish civil society. The most important and democratic of these was the Kirk, and the battle over who should control it, though it seems unutterably arid now, was distinctive. Its impact continued to echo through Scottish society for more than a century.

III

It is difficult to equate today's Kirk, whose sermons on life and morality echo only faintly, with the mighty Church of Scotland of the 1830s. Stand on The Mound in Edinburgh and allow yourself to be overshadowed by the black towers guarding the portal to the Kirk's Assembly Hall, which housed the first meetings of the new parliament, turn and see its view across the city to the shores of Fife, and you see what religion meant to Victorian Scotland – and this was the 'rebel' kirk. Before 1843 the Auld Kirk *was* the Establishment. Its ministers and elders were not just the principal messengers of contemporary morality, but wielded real power through the Kirk's control of the schools, universities and administration of poor relief – the nascent welfare state, then viewed as something primarily religious. All this was challenged by the Disruption, as the cataclysmic 1843 split in the Kirk came to be known.

This was a classic power struggle between church and state. The Kirk's distinct Presbyterianism – the right of congregations to choose their own minister – had in theory been preserved by the Act of Union. Yet in 1712 Westminster restored patronage: the right of a local laird to appoint a minister. Disputes caused by this clash of powers were rarely clear-cut, since a laird's appointee still required the 'call' of a congregation for the appointment to be confirmed. Yet the law was so confused that a strong-willed patron could eventually force a nominee into a parish. This became known as 'intrusion', against which the only remedy for a disgruntled congregation was to break away, no small matter given the minister's powers over parish education and poor relief.

The struggle came to the boil as the Kirk failed to adapt to a rapidly urbanising and industrialising Scotland, and cities and towns where the Kirk's spiritual message and secular hands were absent. Inside the Kirk, an evangelical faction seeking to re-energise the Kirk's mission to such areas wrested power from the conservative establishment and used the Kirk's powers of self-regulation to seek an end to intrusion. But the Scottish courts, subservient to the doctrine of parliamentary supremacy, ruled against these acts while successive Conservative governments, reluctant to cede power to a Kirk which they viewed as dangerously progressive, refused to give up patronage.

This was intolerable to an increasingly radicalised Kirk, which at its General Assembly of 1842, passed the Claim of Right. In essence, it declared that all Acts of Parliament which infringed the rights of the Church of Scotland to govern its own affairs were 'void and null and of no legal force or effect'. This heroically

revolutionary document was rejected by Sir Robert Peel's government, which declared that the courts must arbitrate on the division between matters spiritual where the church held sway, and temporal where the state must prevail. But to the evangelical ministers, the courts were clearly weighted towards the state. Faced with this ruling, which would expel most evangelicals from the Assembly, they were left little option. So in May 1843 they quit, taking with them a third of the Kirk's ministers and members to form the Free Church of Scotland.

The Disruption destroyed the Kirk's claim to be the national church of Scotland, and fatally wounded its capacity to educate the capable and aid the

Figure 1.3 The signing of the Deeds of Demission.
Painting by D. O. Hill. Copyright: Free Church of Scotland. Photograph by George T. Thomson.
One of the great experiments of the nineteenth century which belly-flopped. Hill's collective portrait of the 'rebellion of the pious' was made up from hundreds of calotypes he took with the gifted Robert Adamson. The calotypes were a brilliant record of early Victorian religious, political and intellectual society, the painting an eccentric disaster.

incapable. Presbyterianism became divided between churches and sects competing for the title of the true kirk and too much Scottish energy in the next fifty years became absorbed in abstruse and arid theological disputes. More disastrously, Scotland had lost a national democratic institution with the care

Figure 1.4 The Reverend Thomas Chalmers.
Portrait by Thomas Duncan. Provided by the Scottish National Portrait Gallery.
The contemporary of Thomas Carlyle, Chalmers carried many of the social concerns of the
Enlightenment over into the evangelical revival of the early nineteenth century. A brilliant preacher,
he tried to make the 'Godly Commonwealth' of the Calvinists and Covenanters relevant to the new
industrial society, but the control of the Kirk remained stubbornly in the hands of the landed
classes. The conflict over this was to cause the Disruption in 1843.

of the nation at its heart – worse still, at a time of ferment and agitation in British politics.

IV

Despite the French Revolution, which had so attracted Robert Burns and led to explosive disorder in Ireland in 1798, the nineteenth century had dawned as a Conservative hegemony, in Scotland as well as in England. This was produced by a system in which only wealthy Britons, mainly from the landed classes, had a vote. Out of 2.4 million Scots in 1830, only about 4500 people elected forty-five MPs. Of the towns, only Edinburgh had its own MP, who was elected by the Council, itself filled by co-option. The same went for the other burghs,

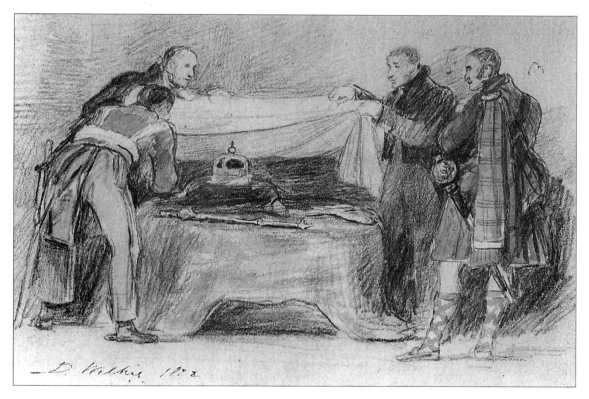

Figure 1.5 Discovery of the Honours of Scotland.
By Sir David Wilkie. Provided by the Scottish National Portrait Gallery.
Sir Walter Scott was terrified at the growth of radicalism. Two years after the 'Battle of Bonnymuir', he was the leading figure in organising George IV's royal visit to Scotland, a feat which he thought would blend the Gaelic and Lowland traditions in mutual loyalty to the King and the constitution. This cleverly anticipated much conservative nationalism but didn't help the old order, which followed the Wizard of the North into the shades in 1832. An incidental benefit, however, was the rediscovery of the Scottish Crown Jewels in the vaults of Edinburgh Castle, where they can still be seen.

voting in groups. Such a system was even worse than that which excluded merchants and industrialists in nearly all British cities, and could not last. In 1820, following the slaughter of demonstrators at 'Peterloo' in Manchester, there occurred the Bonnymuir rising of radical weavers in central Scotland, which the government ruthlessly suppressed. Further agitation, articulated by the young Edinburgh Whigs around the *Edinburgh Review*, prepared the way for the Reform Act of 1832. This widened the franchise, only to about 64000 voters, but this was enough to prise Conservatives out of many Scottish constituencies (which were increased to fifty-three), especially the urban seats, which now had proper electors for the first time. There began a period of Liberal hegemony in Scotland which lasted for half a century.

There was much for the newly enfranchised to agitate over. Liberals saw the Corn Laws, which prohibited imports of grain unless domestic prices rose above a certain level, as a means of putting the profits of landowners above the interests of the urban masses who needed cheap bread. Protests, by pamphlet, demonstration and petition, had been pretty much constant since the Corn Laws had been passed in 1815 and indeed by the time an Anti-Corn Law League was established in Manchester in 1838, free trade had become an article of faith among the Scottish merchant classes. Free trade, indeed, had a resonance in Scotland which went beyond an expression of self-interest, for it accorded with the Presbyterian belief that 'sense an' worth, o'er a' the earth' was to be earned through hard work rather than derived from privilege. The abolition of the Corn Laws in 1846 further undermined the Conservatives, who by then had become the party of rural landed interests.

The still-disenfranchised agitated too. 'Socialists' followed the gospel of Robert Owen of New Lanark; the Chartist movement, founded in England in 1838, gained rapid support in Scotland for its programme which included the demand for universal male suffrage. Scottish Chartism drew on proto-trade union activism amongst coal miners and weavers as well as having substantial middle-class support. Though it faded after 1848, when the rest of Europe heaved with revolution and the Duke of Wellington summoned troops to cow a mass Chartist demonstration in London, it seems to have left a legacy in Scotland of political activism – cooperative, temperance and reform movements – which was unafraid to speak its name.

This period saw burgeoning but still-divided wealth in Scotland, and a population swollen by immigration as well as natural growth. The Conservatives continued to 'manage' the country to preserve the existing order, even compromising with organised labour and evangelicalism, but middle-class hostility steadily reduced their power base. The Liberals, though they were by no means less venal in their abuse of patronage, came to represent radicalism and reform, as in England, but Scottish Liberalism was given a distinctive edge because of the religious issue. But perhaps the most important lesson was learned by the populace – that by the artifices of public debate and demonstration, polemics and pamphleteering, the established upper class could be moved and made to share its power more widely.

V

This discovery appears to have stirred the first flickerings of an orthodox national consciousness. As the cities grew and the problems of ill health, squalor and slums mounted, it became apparent that the Lord Advocate, who was supposed to represent Scotland's interests to the government and the government's interests to Scotland, was overburdened. Whereas Henry Dundas, later Viscount Melville (the man on the column in Edinburgh's St Andrew Square) had been able to handle the post with flair and adroit use of corrupt patronage at the end of the eighteenth century, by the 1820s his family's power was crumbling. Scots complained that they were not being given the legislative time at Westminster needed to keep up with the pace of change, and Scotland's civil administration was seizing up.

Nothing happened in 1848, the year of revolutions, beyond a nasty bread riot in Glasgow. But in 1853 the National Association for the Vindication of Scottish Rights irrupted. A Tory-radical alliance, it sought to improve the Union, not to destroy it. A pamphlet, which sold well, listed a range of grievances, some of which have a familiar ring today; these ranged from the display of English flags to the fact that Scots paid a lot of taxes but got little to spend in return, especially on the universities. It was received disdainfully in London and was rapidly eclipsed by concerns over the Crimean War, a messy business which wound up in 1855, but helpfully provided a plethora of tartan heroes. Scotland again went quiet.

This was when North Britishness reached its zenith. Railways, the communications and engineering wonder of the time, arrived, among them the North British Railway Company which built splendid North British hotels in Edinburgh and Glasgow, names which were only changed in the 1980s. Scots, while they lionised the poetry of Robert Burns, also claimed the novels of Charles Dickens and poetry of Alfred Tennyson as part of their culture. Their own literary dynamo, Thomas Carlyle, announced that the issue of the day was 'the Condition of England Question'. They claimed credit too for the British Empire, counting the contribution of the Enlightenment as part of the reason for British greatness. Queen Victoria gave the royal seal of approval to Scotland, spending every summer after 1848 at Balmoral.

If Scottish nationalism flickered fitfully in this imperial age, new forms of secular Scottish civic society began to emerge from Kirk Disruption. In 1845, poor relief was shifted to parish boards elected by ratepayers and a Board of Supervision was set up in Edinburgh; in 1861, the universities (reformed by an act of 1859) took over school inspection; in 1872, elected parish school boards were set up under a Scotch education department in London. Yet the grievances voiced by the National Association had not gone away and Scottish MPs frequently voiced them, winning a government inquiry in 1869.

VI

What, then, were the values of the Victorian Scots? They were liberals as regards trade, for Scotland thrived on the export industries: cattle, tobacco and linen in the eighteenth century, then cotton, coal, ships and locomotives. But Scots were also aware of the social tensions seething beneath them; one of their favourite metaphors, elaborated by Carlyle, was 'the thin crust of civilisation' that stood between them and social chaos. Their liberalism made them internationalists; they emigrated, as Sir Charles Dilke put it, 'in calculating contentment'. Their 'enlightenment' and their religion, however, the latter in its broadest sense, preoccupied them with what they called 'social police': keeping the working class in order, and providing pathways out of it to strengthen the 'bourgeois' order. Hence the importance of the socialising institutions, the Kirk, the schools, the banks and journalism. All these factors coalesce in the remarkable figure of Hugh Miller, stonemason, later banker and journalist, self-taught geologist and a man comparable to such European figures as Lajos Kossuth, the Hungarian reformer who fought to preserve Magyar culture within the Hapsburg Empire, or Giuseppi Mazzini, ideologist of Italian nationalism. But Miller was forced into the peculiar religious politics of Victorian Scotland, writing polemical tracts against intrusion and patronage while burning with a deeper fire against the landlords who had cleared the glens.

It was this sort of man – though there were women as well, like the pioneer suffragist Marion Reid or the writer Margaret Oliphant – who typified two of the key drives of Victorian Scots democracy: enthusiasm for European nationalism (directed against emperor and pope) and for self-government in the colonial territories. When Kossuth turned up at Hawick station in 1855 he was greeted by locals carrying banners of welcome in his own tongue. These were written by a local 'lad o' pairts', James Murray, then a schoolmaster in the town, who went on to create the *Oxford English Dictionary*. He followed others such as James Wilson, a Hawick hat-maker who moved to London to expand his business and there founded *The Economist* to fight for free trade and individual responsibility in 1843.

In Europe, dictionary-editing was a driving force in 'print-capitalist' nationalism, but Murray enlisted in the service of an imperial or international language.

Figure 1.6 Hugh Miller.
Calotype by D. O. Hill and Robert Adamson. Provided by the Scottish National
Portrait Gallery.
Miller, part Highlander, part Lowlander, was a polymath: geologist, folklorist, banker and
journalist. The sort of man who would have been a moderate nationalist in any European
nation, he was stretched between his British liberalism and strong Scottish and in particular
Highland loyalties. His brilliant autobiography, *My Schools and Schoolmasters*, shows
incipient signs of schizophrenia, which brought an end to his career in 1857, when he
shot himself.

This dualism didn't inhibit but rather transferred nationality. Carlyle moved through Englishness to become more Germanic as he aged. Sir Donald Mackenzie Wallace became the leading authority on Russia, and Professor R. W. Seton-Watson is to this day regarded as a pest in Hungary for going around the Austrian Empire stirring up the Slavs. James Bryce wrote *The American Commonwealth*, the standard treatment of the US constitution almost to Kennedy's day; in 1884 James Lorimer produced the first scheme for a federal Europe. The Scots were, in general, the governing class of the 'white dominions'. They were usually radical in fighting off aristocratic interference from London, though they could be near-racist in expropriating the native people.

VII

Why, then, were they so slow to seek self-government at home? Partly because of a wish to maintain a distance from the demand for Irish home rule which was regarded as toxic to the imperial Britain they did so well out of. But it was also because the route to reform lay in persuading others that reform could be achieved peacefully and would contribute to, not detract from, the greatness of Britain. One of those who had to be so persuaded was William Ewart Gladstone, the grand old man of British Liberalism. Gladstone was born of Scottish parents in Liverpool, where his father had moved to make a fortune in the grain trade. He had many Scottish characteristics, coming from a devout family with a reverence for learning and a concern for the poor which, in Gladstone's case, manifested itself ambivalently with a concern for fallen women. He did not trade on these Scottish roots, however; his opening speech in his Midlothian election campaigns of 1879–80 began: 'I am come among you as a stranger.' This famous campaign, which passed into political history because of Gladstone's prodigious feats of oratory (a two-hour speech to 2000 people without, of course, loudspeakers was pretty standard) and because he was a former prime minister coming back out of retirement, was mainly about foreign policy.

He entered politics in 1837, aged 27, as a Tory, breaking with the Tories over the Corn Laws in 1846 and later joining the Liberals. To modern LibDems (seen from one angle) he was the father of 'home rule all round' – believing that Ireland, Scotland, England and (perhaps) Wales should enjoy domestic legislative autonomy, while participating fully in the imperial parliament at Westminster – but the 'Old Parliamentary Hand' was rarely that straightforward. Government, Gladstone believed, should be frugal and minimal, and his first period as Prime Minister, 1868–74, was unpromising. In 1869, when he received a plea from forty Scottish MPs that the post of Scottish Secretary of State,

Figure 1.7 Professor James Lorimer, 1819–99. Portrait by John Henry Lorimer. Provided by the Scottish National Portrait Gallery. Lorimer was Scotland's 'international man', a pupil of the great Sir William Hamilton who went on to become a pioneer of European international law. A strong cultural nationalist and the great defender of Scots university autonomy, he also pioneered the sensitive restoration of old Scottish houses, a project carried on by his son, the architect Sir Robert Lorimer. His scheme for a European Federal Union (1884) was the first of its kind.

abolished in 1746, should be revived, Gladstone set up an inquiry. It recommended an under-secretary of state at the Home Office, handling political affairs; the Lord Advocate would confine himself to legal matters. Gladstone ignored it. He rejected too an 1872 Commons motion to set up a Select Committee on Scottish Affairs. Though he remained an MP after losing office, he initially intended to quit politics and immerse himself in theological and classical studies. But the collapse of the Ottoman Empire in the Balkans, the war which engulfed the area, the massacres of Christians by the Turks and what he saw as the misguided conduct of foreign policy by Disraeli's Conservative government drew him back in. Partly because his seat in Greenwich was marginal, he was lured to Scotland by the Earl of Rosebery, who thought that Gladstone would revive flagging Scottish Liberal fortunes and that a Liberal administration led by Gladstone would enhance Scotland's (and Rosebery's) position in the British government.

Rosebery, as wealthy and ambitious as he was thin-skinned, was correct on the first count. The Midlothian campaign became electrifying drama, for the seat was held by the Tory Lord Dalkeith, son to the Duke of Buccleuch, custodian of all his father's vested interests. Gladstone's speeches were attended by thousands, printed copies of them sold by the tens of thousands and newspaper accounts were read by millions. They were great, soaring flights of rhetoric, laying out a deeply moral, Christian view of government, placing the citizen at its heart, whose will on any issue, however complex, would be heard and should be obeyed. He laid out the themes of the active citizen and social inclusion, though with lashings of sentiment and platitude, and he caught the mood of the time, for the Liberals and Gladstone returned to government in 1880, winning fifty-three of the sixty Scottish seats.

Disraeli's government had not been idle in Scottish affairs. Political reform became a popular cause in the 1860s. A Scottish National Reform League, demanding that all men should have the vote, attracted 5000 members, including tradesmen and artisans who saw the extended franchise as a way of forcing government to deal with social and industrial problems. It attracted Liberal support too, but both the Liberals and the Tories concentrated on increasing the number of Scottish seats from fifty-three to sixty, each seeing manipulation of these seats as a way of dishing the other. The Liberals won the seats game, but the Tories protected their landed interests by fixing the county qualification of a rateable value of £5 a year for owner-occupiers and £14 for tenants.

Although Gladstone's Midlothian rhetoric invigorated Scottish reformers and energised emerging leaders of the Scottish working class such as Keir Hardie, a union official who became prominent in mining disputes in 1879–81, their support for Gladstone's Liberals received scant reward. Rosebery wasn't offered a Cabinet post and sulked, pestering Gladstone with schemes to enhance Scotland's presence in the government. In 1881, he accepted a junior post at the Home Office but carried on nagging, demanding that Scotland should have a Cabinet minister and a department as did Ireland.

Gladstone, with Irish land on his mind, curtly told him that the Home Secretary was the minister for Scotland, and carried on dealing with Scottish problems in the time-honoured fashion, appointing a commission to inquire into the reasons for crofters' revolts against landlords in the Highlands and

Islands. Scotland was not being specially slighted. Under consistent attack by Irish MPs, his administration was on the ropes; no bills introduced to parliament between 1880 and 1885 for local government reform in Ireland, Scotland and England got through. A scheme for a Local Government Board for Scotland headed by a junior minister was defeated in the House of Lords, provoking outrage. When support for Rosebery's demand for a Scottish Secretary grew to include the Tories at a grandly titled National Convention in Edinburgh in 1884, Gladstone caved in. But his government lapsed into divisions over Ireland and the Sudan and the ensuing brief minority Tory government led by Lord Salisbury had to pass it into law. In 1885, the Duke of Richmond and Gordon, a Tory grandee who thought it a 'quite unnecessary' job, became the first Scottish Secretary since 1746.

Would this quieten the Scottish establishment? The land revolt in Ireland and the first flirtations by British politicians with Irish home rule were finding Scottish echoes. In the Highlands crofters were rebelling against the iniquities of landowners who cleared them from their tiny tenant farms in favour of sheep ranching or deer forests. They wanted at least the same rights as had been granted in Gladstone's 1881 Irish Land Act, and indeed got them in an act passed just before parliament was dissolved. In the 1886 election four crofters MPs were elected, ousting Liberal and Tory lairds, to be joined in parliament by a fifth, the representative of Wick burghs.

Demand was sufficiently strong in Scotland for the Scottish Home Rule Association (SHRA) to be set up in 1886, dedicated as a movement rather than a political party to winning all-party support for the cause. Its leadership was an odd mix of the pragmatic – Dr G. B. Clark, a crofters MP; R. B. Cunninghame Graham, a socialist aristocrat descended from Robert the Bruce and looking every inch the part – and the romantic – John Stuart Blackie, a Celtic revivalist. Keir Hardie was one of its vice-presidents and none other than Ramsay MacDonald, later the first Labour Prime Minister, became secretary.

Despite this array of talent, the SHRA failed to make much of an impact, mainly because the Liberals split when Gladstone decided on Irish home rule. His plan ran quite counter to everything he said in the Midlothian campaign, proposing substantial self-rule for Ireland but nothing for Scotland. Half the Scottish Liberal MPs were appalled (less by Scottish exclusion than by the idea of home rule of any sort) and joined with the Tories to throw out his Government of Ireland Bill. By the 1886 general election, the schism caused in Scottish Liberalism ran deep. Gladstone's later conversion in 1893 to the home-rule-all-round model, now also the cause of the SHRA, couldn't save him and he bowed out.

If Liberalism was wrecked on the rocks of Irish home rule, a new radicalism

Figure 1.8 Professor John Stuart Blackie.
Portrait by Sir George Reid. Provided by the Scottish National Portrait Gallery.
Professor John Stuart Blackie combined Teuton and Gael. A disciple of Carlyle, he was
tireless in agitating for Highland land reform and Gaelic culture.

was born from the wreckage. Home rule was central to the platform of Keir Hardie's fledgling Scottish Labour Party in 1888, and thereafter became a standard fixture of left-wing platforms until the 1950s.

VIII

Yet the overwhelming tenor of Scottish nationalism was cultural rather than political, hinging on the grievances of the successful but subordinate imperial partner that its distinctiveness was not sufficiently recognised. Even in the home rule programme the fads of enthusiasts – for land reform or temperance or getting rid of the established church – counted for more than tackling Scotland's lop-sided industrialisation or the truly hellish living conditions of many of her people.

Cultural influences on the eventual course of Scottish nationalism, however, are perhaps just as important as any of these great shifts in politics. The rise in living standards made the 1880s the first 'consumers' decade', with imported foods, cheap transport, youth movements like the Boys' Brigade and, most significantly for men, sport. Following a fracas in October 1886 at a football match at Hampden Park between Preston North End and Queen's Park – a cup tie, conducted under the auspices of the Football Association (FA) – differences between the FA and its junior organisation, the Scottish Football Association (SFA) came to a head and the SFA disaffiliated itself. If working-class nationalism is influenced more by football than politics, then this may have been more influential than the establishment of the Scottish Office. A definer of nationality had been set up, to the bafflement of federal states such as Germany or Brazil confronted with four midgets from 'these islands', and in due course the country's complex and sometimes menacing football culture developed itself.

The football business shows how complex the culture of Victorian Scotland was. Shared enthusiasm for things like Dickens's novels, sport, choral singing or seaside holidays turned out, on closer inspection, to maintain difference. Dr William Donaldson has reminded us how literate the Victorian Scots were, with their libraries, weekly papers, serials and poems. Scots theatre (much given to lurid adaptations of Walter Scott) was different, and so were Scots choirs. The Burns cult (thanks to Rosebery) went world-wide, and there was a boom in Gaelic culture. The polymath Professor Patrick Geddes even claimed an 1890s Scots Renaissance. Much of this was implicitly nationalist, yet its impact was lessened by the constant tendency to emigrate and to make literature an export article, something that ultimately issued in the commercial sentimentality of the kailyard. When the Americans first started totting up royalties, in 1896, the first-ever 'best-seller' was 'Ian McLaren's' weepie *Beside the Bonnie Brier Bush.*

Figure 1.9 Patrick Geddes, 1856–1932. Portrait by Theodore Houghton. Provided by the Scottish National Portrait Gallery. The pupil of T. H. Huxley, and a thinker and planner of unnerving originality, Geddes toured the world advising the likes of Gandhi and Weizmann while nominally Professor of botany at University College Dundee. In 1896, while based at the Outlook Tower in Edinburgh's Lawnmarket, he proclaimed the Scottish Renaissance. This may have been slightly premature, but he was still there to support MacDiarmid's efforts in the 1920s.

Home rule was now a periodic response to problems in the Scottish economy, though it didn't have the connection that existed in Ireland with the land issue. Only 10 per cent of Scots lived from agriculture (and most of these were labourers rather than peasants) while over 70 per cent of the Irish depended on it. The demand for home rule began to revive in the early 1900s with the foundation of the Young Scots' Society, on the left wing of the Liberal Party, but its cause wasn't helped by the fact that after a nasty slump in 1906–8 the traditional economy bounced back, reaching record production levels in all main branches in 1913. Yet the established order of the Scottish shipyards and engineering works was under threat from the increased competition of rivals, particularly Germany and the United States, and the importation of new practices and technology from these places by manufacturers who believed that a confrontation with their labour force could not be postponed. The Edwardian period, beneath its rich, almost cloying topping of golf hotels and crack expresses, avant-garde architecture and painting, and a comfortable middle-class

Figure 1.10 Glasgow's Scottish Historical Exhibition of 1911. Photograph provided by T. and R. Annan & Sons Ltd, Glasgow. The purpose of the exhibition was to endow a Scots history chair at the university, proof of cultural revival of the national cause. (The English Professor of history, Dudley Medley, didn't believe the subject existed.) But it also had a high kailyard content and exposed the country's over-reliance on the heavy industries.

Figure 1.11 Ramsay MacDonald, 1866–1937.
Portrait by Ambrose MacEvoy. Provided by the Scottish National Portrait Gallery.
MacDonald started his political career as a Scottish Home Rule Association organiser. His wife
Margaret was a distant relative of W. E. Gladstone, and during the 1890s he set his sights on a
Liberal seat. Frustration here made him an effective secretary of the Labour Representation
Committee founded by the Trades Union Congress (TUC) and the man whose secret negotiations
with W.E.'s son, Herbert Gladstone, led to Labour's breakthrough in 1906. In his sad twilight as
National Labour Prime Minister, 1931–5, when his 'minder' was John Buchan, he reverted
romantically to his home rule past. The Scottish business élite protested vociferously in the
'Ragman's Roll' of 1934.

lifestyle, was made increasingly unstable by mounting industrial unrest in the mines and docks and on the railways.

Keir Hardie's Scottish Labour Party had essentially been an equivalent to Parnell's Irish party, giving home rule a priority. After 1893, as the Independent Labour Party, it was more Westminster-oriented and this attracted the unions.

Figure 1.12 George Douglas Brown. Etching by James Pryde, 1900. Provided by the Scottish National Portrait Gallery. *The House with the Green Shutters* (1900) gave kailyard stereotypes a roasting and prefigures the national self-criticism that MacDiarmid was to release with *The Drunk Man* a quarter-century later, though he referred to it rather slightingly in relationship to the kailyard as 'the same thing disguised as its opposite'. Douglas Brown's sharp portrayal of Scottish society owes much to John Galt, whom he helped edit, but also to his own 'marginality' as the illegitimate son of an Irish farm servant.

It was MacDonald's skill as a negotiator which brought about a secret pact with the Liberals and partial success in 1906. Its home rule commitment faded but the Scottish radicals patronised Tom Johnston's weekly *Forward*, with its socialism, radical liberalism and home rule. Many young writers, painters and artists were attracted to the propaganda of socialism, including Edwin Muir adrift on the urban tide of Glasgow, or John MacDougall Hay who assaulted the greed of nineteenth-century employers in *Gillespie* (1914). They generally assumed that socialism would be accomplished within the frame of a Scottish state, but at the same time their ideals were essentially internationalist. Under the Liberal government of Campbell-Bannerman and Asquith home rule motions were regularly carried, but those which really mattered concerned Ireland. After the constitutional crisis of 1909–10 an Irish bill was inevitable. Ulster Protestants, organised by Sir Edward Carson and the Scots-Canadian Andrew Bonar Law, campaigned against it, invoking the spirit of the Covenanters of 1638 and threatening violent resistance. Had Ulster exploded, could Scotland, with its substantial communities of Catholic and Protestant immigrants, have stayed unaffected? But, on 28 June 1914, other explosions – at Sarajevo – determined the way the world went.

CHAPTER TWO

Red Flag and Saltire

Noo come a' ye at hame wi' freedom
Never heed what the corbies cry o' doom.
In ma hoose a' the bairns o' Adam
Will find breid, barley-bree an' pentit room.
When MacLean meets wi' freens in Springburn
A' the roses and geans'll turn tae bloom,
An the black boy frae yont Nyanga
Dings the fell gallows o' the burgers doon.

Hamish Henderson, 'The Freedom Come-all-ye'

I

World War I marked the sharpest of breaks. Before it, Scotland was at the centre of a huge and productive, though deeply inegalitarian, Atlantic economy which didn't just demand ships and locomotives, coal and engineers; it was the linkage between the Old World – the enormous economic and military strength of the European powers – and the still-immature and unpredictable United States. By 1922 these statuses would be reversed. Europe was diminished through wartime exhaustion and sheer economic collapse, though no less unstable. America continued to prosper for a few years more, and then, in 1929, with its banks heavily involved in Europe, it collapsed as well. Pre-1914, Scotland had benefited from the transatlantic synergy; Glasgow was an essential link in the chain of trade and production, frenetically busy building the ships which carried goods from and to its docks. Its unemployment was negligible and well below the British average. After 1921, unemployment rose above the British average and stayed there, thus giving harsh reality to the enduring (poor) North/(rich) South divide in UK society and politics.

Even without the collapse of sea-borne prosperity, the war hit the country hard. Casualties in Scotland were higher than for Britain as a whole (some computations suggest by as much as 50 per cent) despite the numbers of skilled men in 'reserved' occupations. With bases like Rosyth, Scapa and Invergordon, the country was itself in the front line, something conveyed in John Buchan's 'condition of Britain' thriller *Mr Standfast* (1919). Out of the flux of war, empire and a burgeoning capitalism to which Glasgow was pivotal came two things: a great democratisation, which upped the electorate by a factor of three but wasn't much noticed, and a new and confrontational politics, which was.

Red Clydeside is still iconic in British socialism. Its figures have intrigued generations of the left, among them Gordon Brown, who owns up in his biography *Maxton* (1987) to a teenage fascination with the man. In 1979, the Soviet Union issued a stamp in honour of John MacLean. In a 1989 parliamentary by-election in Glasgow Central, Alex Neil, the SNP candidate, claimed the inheritance by calling himself and Jim Sillars, who had recently won Glasgow Govan, the 'new Clydesiders'.

Red Clydeside assumed mythic status because in 1919 Lloyd George's government feared Bolshevik revolution was erupting on the Clyde two years after it had toppled the Tsar. It deployed tanks and troops on the streets of a British

THE TRAMP TRUST UNLIMITED.

Sandy Ross   Jas. D. MacDougall
Peter Marshall   John MacLean M.A.   Harry McShane

Figure 2.1 John MacLean (1879–1923) and his socialist missionaries, 1922.
Photograph provided by the Scottish National Portrait Gallery. Copyright: *The Herald*.
John MacLean MA (the MA was never absent) was effectively the founder of Scottish working-class political education. His rejection of Moscow control of the Communist Party, and admiration of James Connolly (1866–1916) led him to ally with the romantic nationalist and Gaelic revivalist Ruaraidh Erskine of Mar. Later socialists and nationalists like MacDiarmid and Hamish Henderson tended to present him as a figure similar to Connolly, not always successfully.

Figure 2.2 James Maxton (1885–1946), 1930.
Portrait by Sir John Lavery. Provided by the Scottish National Portrait Gallery. By courtesy of
Felix Rosenstiel's Widow & Son Ltd, London, on behalf of the Estate of Sir John Lavery.
'He didn't just preach the revolution, he looked it!' Maxton led the International Labour Party
(ILP) out of the Labour Party in 1932. His Glasgow colleagues – John McGovern and
Campbell Stephen – followed him but, although committed to home rule, they parted from
most of their Scottish rank and file and regarded world revolution and anti-fascism as more
important. The brilliant orator and passionate humanitarian is captured in Sir John Lavery's
portrait, but Maxton's indolence and lack of strategy were fatal flaws.

city (the only time tanks have ever been so used) to suppress what was called the Forty-Hour Strike. In fact, Red Clydeside was a mixture of the noble – protest against usurious rents – and the ignoble – efforts by skilled workers to prevent the infiltration of their crafts by unskilled men and women, thus hampering production of munitions for the front line.

II

This was a time when a great tectonic shift in British politics had begun – from the Liberals to the Labour Party – and a Scottish political dimension started to assert itself more prominently. The Scottish Liberals, whom Friedrich Engels described in the 1890s as the most advanced bourgeoisie in the world, had now to struggle to represent both the middle and the working classes. The landowners, against whom all urban-dwellers could be united in the name of progressive reform (the Crofters Party rejoined the Liberals in 1892), became a less convincing bogeyman for those who toiled in the mines and factories than were the owners of these enterprises. For the douce businessmen and lawyers who in 1910 held fifty-eight of Scotland's seventy-two seats – a representation biased in favour of the countryside – the future was worrying.

Trade unionism was on the march. In the 1890s, there were around 150000 union members, mostly concentrated in the engineering and shipbuilding trades and in the Glasgow area. Very early, Scottish trade unionism took on a distinctive tinge as the Scots rebelled against an attempt by the craft unions to use the newly founded Trades Union Congress (TUC) to exclude locality-based Trades Councils which represented unskilled workers. This was politically inspired; the Trades Councils were seen as socialist and a threat to Liberalism, with which the TUC leadership was identified and for which they had been denounced as collaborators with the ruling classes by Keir Hardie in 1887. In 1897, the Scottish Trades Union Congress (STUC), embracing the Trades Councils, was set up and promptly began work aimed at securing independent Labour representation in parliament. This did not bear much fruit. Only two Labour MPs were elected in 1906 and the first election in 1910; three were successful in the second 1910 election. One of these was in Dundee, a two-member seat in which voters had two votes, thus allowing them to vote Labour and Liberal. The Liberal who benefited from an endorsement from his Labour colleague in the second 1910 election was Winston Churchill, no less, who repudiated the debt, as Home Secretary, by refusing to meet the STUC. Trade union activism, however, became more aggressive. One estimate is that there were seventy industrial disputes in west Central Scotland in 1912, including a national strike by miners for a minimum wage. Employers reacted by forming associations to resist industrial militancy.

III

War brought new tensions into this restive society. Working men responded enthusiastically to the call to arms; about a quarter of Scottish miners are reckoned to have joined up and an entire battalion was recruited from the staff of Glasgow Corporation's tram department. However, the heavy industrial employers, gearing up for wartime production, needed more rather than fewer workers. Men and women flooded into the city, perhaps as many as 20 000, from all over Britain, Ireland and even America. Housing was a big problem; even before the war half of Glasgow lived in one- or two-room flats. Rents (there was little public housing) started to rise, by up to 24 per cent in Govan and Fairfield. In 1915, tenants started withholding rents, with women, many of whose husbands were at the front, to the fore.

As there were similar movements in Birmingham, alarmed Liberal government ministers began drawing up a rent control bill to which they had to overcome opposition from Conservative coalition ministers. When Lloyd George, then munitions minister, lent his support, progress began to be made. Before it could be passed, a factor summonsed eighteen defaulting tenants to the sheriff court to have their wages arrested. Shipyard and munitions workers downed tools and many thousands marched on the court to demonstrate. Inside, the sheriff made his hostility to the case known and the factor, who cannot have been insensible to the much greater fury outside, withdrew his case. A rent control bill was passed six days later, starting a Scottish tradition of controlled rents which lasted until the 1980s, and incidentally destroying the philanthropic *rentiers* (but *rentiers* none the less) who sustained municipal Liberalism. But the bill brought Lloyd George no gratitude in Glasgow.

Two days after the passage of the bill, on Christmas Day 1915 (not then a public holiday in Scotland), he spoke at a public meeting in the city. The meeting was bedlam and Lloyd George, who thought the city 'ripe for revolution', could hardly be heard. He suppressed the socialist newspaper *Forward*, which printed a lively account, complete with hecklers knocking the Welsh wizard's oratory to bits. In fact, the meeting was not much interested in rents; the issue was the influx of unskilled workers, many of them women, into factories to do work which had hitherto been the preserve of skilled workers. This was known as dilution and Lloyd George regarded it as essential to raising production.

Employers, by and large tactless managers, thirsted for dilution. Some demanded that the government put factories under military discipline. The trade unions were not well organised to meet this challenge. In February 1915, the Amalgamated Society of Engineers refused to authorise a strike by 10 000 engineering workers seeking a pay rise. Factory officials reacted by organising the Central Labour Withholding Committee, later to become the Clyde Workers

Committee (CWC). Though the CWC was more concerned with pay, working conditions and resisting the conscription of industrial labour, Whitehall viewed it as a cell of revolutionaries.

Led by David Kirkwood, Arthur MacManus, Willie Gallacher and others, the CWC organised resistance to dilution, their fear being that employers would use dilution to bring in cheap labour and force pay down. How much of this was socialist? Even in January 1916, when the suppression of the *Worker* provoked a rash of strikes, not all shops joined in. In March the government struck back, muttering about reports of German agents. It used wartime laws to deport nine shop stewards, including Kirkwood, from Glasgow to Edinburgh. A protest demonstration was held on Glasgow Green, addressed by the lank school-teacher who would become the image of Scottish socialism, James Maxton. 'Not a rivet should be struck on the Clyde until the deported engineers are restored to their families,' he declared. He too was arrested. But reports of the altogether bloodier confrontation of Easter 1916 in Dublin came quite unexpectedly.

Shorn of their leaders and spurred by some exemplary fines imposed by the courts, the strikers were back at work within two weeks. Uneasy ways of living with dilution, which was introduced factory by factory under the oversight of government-appointed commissioners, were found and the CWC was broken. After 1916, industrial militancy faded, only to re-emerge at the end of the war.

IV

Rivalry and division marked the new politics of the left. Keir Hardie's Scottish Labour Party had proved too weak to make an impact and in 1894 dissolved itself into the Independent Labour Party (ILP), formed the previous year in Bradford as a British organisation and the political means of achieving parliamentary representation of the industrial wings of the Labour movement. Efforts to make this two-winged bird of socialism fly in Scotland were bedevilled by rivalries, between the Labour Representation Committee (LRC) and the Scottish Workers Representation Committee, which both sought the affiliations of Scottish trade unions. The LRC won, becoming the Labour Party in 1906 and eventually recognising the difficulties of political organisation in Scotland with the establishment of a Scottish Advisory Council in 1913.

Other groups were much more revolutionary. The British Socialist Party, formed in 1911, was inspired in Scotland by John MacLean, a teacher and self-taught Marxist capable of moving thousands with his oratory. Another was the Socialist Labour Party, founded by James Connolly in 1902. Connolly was born in Edinburgh and was *Forward*'s Irish correspondent; he was shot by a British firing squad as a leader of the Easter Rising.

The veteran Clydesider Harry McShane noted that politics evicted 'vital religion' from the oratory of Glasgow Green about 1906. But it remained true to the secessionist spirit, which made for little electoral progress. Still, the socialist belief that 'means of production, distribution and exchange should be owned by the whole people for the benefit of the people' was conquering minds. Books, such as Tom Johnston's *Our Noble Families*, a broadside against inherited privilege; papers like *Forward*, *Vanguard* and the *Worker*; lectures in the open air and evening classes held by John MacLean and others, all spread the new ideology. Glasgow's May Day march attracted only 10 000 in 1916 but over 70 000 the following year.

The war split the left. Lewis Grassic Gibbon got the mood in the distant Mearns, where the socialist Chae Strachan becomes a fire-eating anti-German, while Long Rob believes the whole thing is the work of the bosses. The industrial militants took the latter line and these ideas grew with war-weariness and the impact of the Russian Revolution. Imprisonment of leaders like Maxton and MacLean became riskier. MacLean's second term of imprisonment in 1918 caused such huge protests that he was released to great celebrations after serving only seven months of a five-year sentence.

MacLean arrived back in Glasgow from Peterhead Prison in December 1918 to a city whose workforce feared that demobilisation and the ending of munitions production would bring mass unemployment. They demanded that the working week be cut, from fifty-four to forty hours. The CWC, now reborn as the Ways and Means Committee, organised meetings of shop stewards in January 1919 to run a general strike from Monday, 27 January. General it wasn't, but some 40 000 workers struck. Emmanuel Shinwell, of the Glasgow Trades Council, tried to shut down places which refused to strike, such as the municipally owned power stations and tramways. Shinwell warned the Lord Provost of more drastic action, and called a demonstration in George Square in front of the City Chambers. On the morning of Friday, 31 January, the square filled with a sea of flat caps. Trouble came when the police drew batons and made several charges. The demonstrators fought back, some flinging lemonade bottles. But that was really that.

For strike and riot to be seen as near-revolution was entirely due to the government's over-reaction. The Cabinet was solemnly informed by Robert Munro, the Scottish Secretary, that this was a Bolshevist rising. Willie Gallacher later said that they ought to have got the crowd to march on Maryhill Barracks and get the soldiers there to mutiny. Maybe sensing the feelings of local soldiers, Munro sent troops and six tanks from London by overnight train, to be stationed in the Cattle Market. With Glasgow effectively under military control, the strike petered out within two weeks. The trade union leaders were tried and three got shortish sentences.

V

Red Clydeside was not about revolution but about pay and work. While Lenin appointed John MacLean as Bolshevik Consul in Glasgow in 1918, MacLean's calls to socialist struggle were mostly ignored, as was his attempt – applauded by later nationalists – to emulate Connolly and forge a revolutionary alliance for a Scottish Workers' Republic with the aristocratic Gaelic enthusiast Ruaraidh Erskine of Mar. The failure to politicise was shown by the general election of 1918. Labour broke through with fifty-nine MPs, but only seven of these were from Scotland, and only one of these in Glasgow, where Neil McLean won Govan. The Lloyd George coalition's appeal to patriotism beat socialism, less because of propaganda about the latter's devilish and alien qualities, than because few troops had returned in time to vote.

The 1922 election was rather different. This time, Labour doubled its vote in the city to 42 per cent and won ten of Glasgow's fifteen seats. The new Tory Prime Minister, Andrew Bonar Law, narrowly escaped defeat in Glasgow Central. Rising unemployment in the post-war recession played a part in this. So too did the truly shocking housing conditions in 'the city of dreadful night'. Controlled rents meant that it was uneconomic to build new housing, while low wages meant rents could not be significantly increased without adding to the existing deprivation. As yet the 1919 Housing Act, which enabled central government to subsidise the building of public housing by local government, had not made a difference. Against this background, Labour dug itself into municipal politics. Their old link to Liberals via Irish home rule now broken (Glasgow was an important centre of Irish Republican Army (IRA) organisation in the 'Troubles' of 1918–21), Catholics were heavily drawn to the Labour Party, in part thanks to the work of one of the Clydeside socialists, John Wheatley, whose Catholic Socialist Society preached the new politics to the mainly Irish-origin unskilled workers. The position of Catholics in Scottish society had also been solidified by the 1918 Education Act, which granted state finance through local councils to local schools.

So in 1922, Red Clydeside came to parliamentary maturity, joining the mainstream tide which saw 142 Labour MPs elected that year, displacing the Liberals as the main opposition to Bonar Law's Tories. A vast crowd, wildly estimated to be anything between 40 000 and 120 000, flocked to Glasgow St Enoch Station to cheer the new MPs off. They included Manny Shinwell, elected in Linlithgow; Tom Johnston, who won West Stirling; George Hardie, brother of Keir Hardie who had died in 1915; Davie Kirkwood, triumphant in Dumbarton: James Maxton, victor at last in Glasgow Bridgeton; and John Wheatley, winner of Glasgow Shettleston. The crowd roared out the Red Flag, the International, Jerusalem and the Twenty-Fourth Psalm, beloved of the Covenanters:

Then Israel
May say, and that truly,
If that the Lord
Had not our cause maintained
When cruel men
Against us furiously
Rose up in wrath
To make of us their prey . . .

The MPs orated, promising to work unceasingly for decent pay and conditions in industry, to eradicate monopoly and avarice, and to have regard for the weak and those stricken by disease. Writing about the scene half a century later, Gordon Brown commented with evident pride:

It may not have turned out to be the Scottish equivalent of July 1789 in France, or October 1917 in Russia, but it still ranks as the Scottish Labour Movement's finest hour.

But was the socialist future to be through parliament, through industrial action or through Scotland? The Red Clydesiders had spoken of soon coming back with a parliament; the Triple Alliance of railwaymen, miners and transport workers was still in being, and the 'industrial' way wasn't closed off until the failure of the General Strike in 1926.

VI

Against this left-wing radicalism was a 'liberal' national solution: enthusiasm for small ethnic nations and international bodies for open diplomacy. Both had Scots origins; the nationalist tradition has already been referred to, but the impulses which led to the foundation of the League of Nations had their roots in the 'international public right' which pioneers such as Gladstone and Lorimer had represented. The essential draft for the League had come from the hand of James, Viscount Bryce of Dechmont, prime authority on the American constitution and former ambassador to Washington. The impulse given to ethnic nationalism had marked the European settlement at the Versailles peace conference and strengthened the demand for home rule, but nationalism wasn't to be, any more than the League, one of Europe's success stories.

Nevertheless, events like the Easter Rising in Dublin and the Versailles Treaty triggered the remarkable renaissance of Scots literature in the 1920s, under Christopher Murray Grieve (better known as 'Hugh MacDiarmid'), a man in whom the mighty smash-and-grab intellect of Carlyle was combined with a

"SOUVENIR OF THE GREAT STRIKE 1926"

"ON PATROL"

Fraternally yours,
John Bird

Figure 2.3 The General Strike, 1926: a 'miners' militiaman on horseback in Fife.
Photograph provided by the Trustees of the National Library of Scotland.
A posed photograph and something of a joke, contrasting the miners with the mounted police who opposed
them. The strike lasted only nine days; the miners' lockout dragged on until November. MacDiarmid saw it as
the chance for the Scottish working class to remake itself. Instead it shifted trade union strategy to back political,
and especially Labour Party, activity.

rare lyrical gift. This didn't lead to straightforward politics. In MacDiarmid,
radical socialism co-existed with something close to his friend Ezra Pound's
mixture of fascism and social credit. Other Renaissance men blended everything
from social Catholicism to down-the-line Stalinism. But the circumstances of
Scotland and the collapse of the industrial machine that had settled career
questions for a couple of generations opened out politics and literature as
surrogate forms of self-development.

In the debris left by war and recession, though, political nationalism was a
feeble flame. One votary was Roland Eugene Muirhead, owner of a Renfrewshire
tannery company. A socialist who financed Tom Johnston's *Forward* and
member of the ILP, he also paid for the revival of the Scottish Home Rule
Association in 1918. Muirhead believed in the SHRA as a movement, that it
would bind support from across the political spectrum in a common cause, then
defined on the later Gladstonian model as Scottish self-rule over domestic
administration within a Britain whose parliament would be concerned with
imperial affairs. Its support came mainly from the ILP and the trade unions.

The failure of Scottish MPs to support home rule in a 1919 Commons debate led Muirhead to believe that a National Convention representing various Scottish interests should be created to exert pressure on Westminster.

Despite the election in 1924 of a minority Labour government under Ramsay MacDonald, the sundering of the Liberals decisively tipped the balance of Scottish MPs' opinion against home rule. A bill introduced that year by one of the Clydeside MPs, George Buchanan, fell amid scenes of uproar in the Commons. MacDonald, aware of his precarious grasp on power amid pressing economic problems, was loth to press the issue. The SHRA, meanwhile, had become dominated by the Labour Party, by then the only political party supporting the cause. But, to the frustration of nationalist elements in Muirhead's National Convention which had been formed in 1924, its Labour members were hostile to any ideas of pressing for home rule by means which would cause trouble for the government. Among the frustrated nationalist members, talk of forming a nationalist party began to grow.

Muirhead forced the split in the SHRA into the open when he announced in 1928 that he would stand for parliament as a home rule candidate. In April that year, discussions between various nationalist organisations in the Convention – the Scottish National League, the Scottish National Movement, the National Party Group, the Glasgow University Student Nationalists Association and SHRA nationalists – resolved to create the National Party of Scotland (NPS) to contest elections on the platform of Scottish self-government. Its founding statement was to find echoes in the SNP's rhetoric seventy years later in the 1997 Scottish parliament elections:

> Entirely independent of London-controlled parties, the National Party's appeal is to every Scotsman and woman without distinction of class or creed.

Muirhead joined the new party and urged every nationalist in the SHRA to follow him, which most did.

The NPS had literary lions in its den, although their political contributions were fairly inept, enabling opponents to deride it as a 'mutual admiration society for struggling poets and novelists'. McDiarmid was then writing his finest lyrics, but his politics were all over the place, from the socialist idealism of 'The Ballad of the General Strike' to the ominous 'Plea for a Scottish Fascism'. Muirhead concluded that he was out for a Celtic dictatorship. Compton Mackenzie, thought of today as the amiable author of Highland comedies such as *Whisky Galore* but whose fine earlier works inspired Scott Fitzgerald, dabbled at tedious length with a sort of neo-Jacobitism. There was much enthusiasm for social credit, the arcane anti-bank ideology preached by the Dundee-born

Figure 2.4 Sir Compton Mackenzie.
Portrait by Robert Heriot Westwater. Provided by the Scottish National Portrait Gallery.
Mackenzie, born Montagu Compton in Hartlepool in 1883, made himself into the Grand Old
Man of Scottish nationalism after he was elected Rector of Glasgow University on a National
Party ticket in 1932, though in certain respects his face, albeit impressive, didn't fit. He was a
Catholic convert, when most Nats tended to be Protestant; his politics were more conservative
than MacDiarmid's (Oswald Mosley was a friend) and their main exposition, in the first chapter
of *The North Wind of Love* (1940) shows them far removed, in their neo-Jacobitism, from
Scottish reality. For nearly half a century he and Wendy Wood (q.v.) seemed to personify
romantic Scottish nationalism, though persistent rumours suggested that behind both of them
stood Mackenzie's old bosses in MI5.

engineer Major C. H. Douglas: 'Like childbirth without pain, and even more intriguingly, without a child,' was Lewis Grassic Gibbon's cool response. Lewis Spence, the first NPS candidate, was an expert on Atlantis. At an angle to the myth-men was Eric Linklater, who stood for the NPS in a 1933 parliamentary by-election in East Fife, later using the experience in a novel, *Magnus Merriman*, and there discovering the 'calm indifference of ignorance' of the middle classes to the Nationalist cause.

Fortunately for the NPS, it recruited some able politicians, one being John MacCormick, who cut his teeth in ILP student politics at Glasgow University and was intent on parliamentary pragmatism. The party's early forays into elections were less than startling, the best performance being a 14 per cent share

Figure 2.5 Founding fathers of the National Party of Scotland, 1929.
Photograph provided by Gordon Wright Photo Library.
The Duke of Montrose, Compton Mackenzie, Robert Bontine Cunninghame-Graham, Hugh MacDiarmid, James Valentine and John MacCormick on the occasion of Cunninghame-Graham standing against Prime Minister Stanley Baldwin for the rectorship of Glasgow University. He almost won. Did Lenin say that you couldn't make an omelette without breaking egos?

of the vote gained by MacCormick in Inverness in the 1931 election. As Magnus Merriman found out, the party's 'diverse enthusiasms for Communism, pacifism, vegetarianism, poetic non-conformity, and economic heresy' impaired the presentation of a united front.

VII

Politically, these were deeply confusing times. Quite apart from the still-reverberating Liberal disruption, Ramsay MacDonald's decision in 1931 to form a coalition government with the Tories horrified the mass of socialists, particularly after a Liberal-Tory alliance wiped out all but seven Labour MPs in the subsequent election. MacDonald reverted at least rhetorically to his home rule origins, probably inspired by the enigmatic figure of John Buchan MP, who acted as his minder and thought the Scots should have a bash at setting up a legislature, even if it flopped. Scottish business and local government came down on any such idea like a ton of bricks.

Linklater, in *Magnus Merriman*, captured the confusion perfectly:

> (The voters) were asked to elect a Conservative who had lately been a Liberal; a Liberal who for forty years had been a Conservative; a Socialist who condemned the policy of the existing Socialist government; an Independent Conservative who divided his allegiance between high tariffs and Lady Mercy Cotton [a press baroness]; and a Scottish Nationalist who was apparently at odds with many other members of his party.

The Irish home rule question might have exited with Irish independence, but most Scottish Tories disavowed the name Conservative and continued to campaign as Unionists.

MacCormick resolved to clarify the Nationalist position by expelling 'extremists' and recruiting some better-known names. The need for this became urgent when a rival nationalist party, the Scottish Party, appeared in 1932. It was formed by Glasgow Tories who wanted to fuse Conservatism with nationalism in a devolution platform but who were repelled by the Celticism of the NPS, and picked up a lot of support from former Liberals, whose party had split three ways. The Scottish Party had a repellent side too, however, with some of its recruits being anti-Roman Catholic and anti-Irish.

This was part of a most unsavoury phase in Scottish politics. In 1923, the General Assembly of the Church of Scotland approved a report calling on the government to stem the tide of Irish immigration, stating that such immigrants 'cannot be assimilated and absorbed into the Scottish race'. In the economic slump of the early 1930s when the Scottish unemployment rate soared to nearly

30 per cent, employers and trade unions connived at keeping Catholics out of jobs while Protestant parties won up to a third of the vote at municipal elections in Glasgow and Edinburgh. Muirhead, like the chief Labour home ruler, the Reverend James Barr, was genuinely ecumenical, but admitted that nationalism was a Protestant cause.

MacCormick got rid of McDiarmid, who had tried to set up a paramilitary nationalist organisation, and others who became vituperative in their abuse of him. He persuaded the party that independence meant Scottish self-government within the British Commonwealth, and cooperation with England in defence and foreign policy. This concession to devolutionists was opposed by NPS fundamentalists. But their feet were knocked from under them when Linklater came bottom of the poll in the East Fife by-election, behind even an agricultural unionist sponsored by Lord Beaverbrook, proprietor of *The Daily Express* and the Lady Mercy Cotton character in *Magnus Merriman*.

Urgency was given to protracted negotiations over merging the parties by the imminence of a by-election in Kilmarnock where it seemed the two parties would end up fighting each other. They managed to agree only on a joint candidate, Sir Alexander MacEwen of the Scottish Party. NPS members' suspicions that the merger was driving them away from independence towards a devolutionary stance, which had put a brake on MacCormick's enthusiasm for a merger, were overridden when MacEwen polled 17 per cent of the vote, admittedly in the absence of a Tory candidate. In April 1934, the new Scottish National Party (SNP) was unveiled, with MacEwen as chairman and a devolutionary rather than an independence platform.

It arrived precisely when enthusiasm for home rule was waning. The scars of depression were deep and even an old home ruler like Tom Johnston, who lost his seat in 1931 because of the intervention of the NPS, sarcastically remarked that there was little point in having a Scottish parliament 'to administer an emigration system, a glorified Poor Law and a graveyard'. More evil and threatening forms of nationalism were arising – Nazism in Germany, fascism in Italy and Spain, imperial nationalism in Japan – all aggressively militaristic and far removed from the SNP's democratic ideals but none the less casting a darkening shadow over them.

VIII

This was clearly a time when Unionist arguments that there was more collective strength in a united Britain had much force. Indeed the Scottish Unionist Association, under which name the Tories now sailed, had gathered force, winning thirty-seven of the seventy-one Scottish seats in 1935. Unionism in 1930s Scotland can be seen as an early example of the 'one-nation' Conservatism that would serve the Tories well in 1950s Britain. Capitalism had to be fettered in the national interest, for example, through the Special Areas Act which introduced subsidies to encourage industrial development, through public sector housebuilding programmes, and through an Agricultural Wages Board which set a minimum wage for farm workers.

Unionism had some outstanding characters: the Duchess of Atholl, Scotland's first woman MP, elected in Kinross and West Perthshire in 1932 and a vigorous opponent of appeasement; Robert Boothby, MP for East Aberdeenshire from 1924 to 1958, who despised *laissez-faire* capitalism; and John Buchan, novelist and MP for Scottish Universities from 1926 to 1935, when he was appointed Governor-General of Canada. It also produced one remarkable politician: Walter Elliot, Secretary of State from 1935 to 1938.

Elliot, scientist, bon viveur and coiner of the phrase 'democratic intellectualism' – 'too damn clever for his own good' in the eyes of many Tories, Churchill included – not only presided over an emollient Toryism, but laid claim to nationalism as well. Under his tenure a great Empire Exhibition was held in Glasgow's Bellahouston Park in 1938, a chest-swelling showcase for

Figure 2.6 The Scottish Pavilion South.
From the *Official Guide, Empire Exhibition, Scotland, 1938*.
A landmark of the Art Deco ensemble designed by Basil Spence, Jack Coia and other bright young Scots architects under Tommy Tait's leadership. The Empire Exhibition was organised by Walter Elliot. 'Never a dull moment, and never an angry word,' remembered his widow. He was the ideas man of Scottish politics and Secretary of State, 1935–8. Elliot was, like Tom Johnston, a great 'doer'; he left behind him the Scottish Economic Committee, the Scottish Special Housing Association, and Film of Scotland. Meeting the Young Communist Hamish Henderson at the Paris Exhibition of 1937 he made out a case for Glasgow outdoing Paris, which it probably did.

Figure 2.7 John Buchan (1875–1940) as High Commissioner to the General Assembly, 1934.
Photograph provided by the Trustees of the National Library of Scotland.
The High Commissioner and his entourage. A year later Buchan would go to Canada as Governor-General and a lot more of the same. Although Buchan himself was from the more 'democratic' Free Church, his party represented a cross-section of an upper class which increasingly invested and lived in the South.

Scotland and Scottish industry. Of longer-term significance was the reorganisation and streamlining of Scottish administration, much of which was conducted by a hodgepodge of boards which were answerable to the Treasury for their money and staff and not to the Scottish Secretary, whose post had been elevated to full Cabinet rank in 1926 but whose bureaucrats were mostly in London.

This preoccupied John Buchan in a 1932 Commons debate, not long after Glasgow students had elected Compton Mackenzie as Rector; such contests were still viewed seriously as a barometer of political feeling. Buchan complained that Scotland's affairs were being so mishandled that the country would soon have nothing distinctive to show to the world. The Scottish Office should be moved to Edinburgh from Whitehall, housed in a building symbolising Scottish nationhood, he declared, so that Scotland could be seen to have 'her own compact and organic system of government'.

This vision was duly realised in 1939 with the opening of St Andrew's House, Tommy Tait's imposing pile commanding the southern crags of Calton Hill. The Scottish Secretary now had a civil service machine, divided into four departments – Home (law, justice and local government), Agriculture, Health and Education – which could rival those of Whitehall, bring coherence to the government's administration of Scotland, and provide a civil service career for Scots who were ambitious to make a mark on Scotland's public infrastructure. But by the time Buchan's symbol of nationhood opened for business, war had broken out.

What endured from the inter-war years was the realisation that a community, whether nation or region, consisted of something more than statistics of production. Even unionists accepted that the country's industrialisation had been one-sided, and that the costs of this development were exposed when the economy stopped growing. How were persistent ill-health, pollution, an appalling housing problem and unbalanced industrial development to be overcome? In one way the weakness of the economy led to integration with the South, a trend accepted by the Clydesiders which dimmed their home rule zeal. The replacement of administrative boards which were broadly representative with civil service departments fitted this pattern, although it did broaden the scope for Scottish policy-making.

But these solutions had strong cultural-nationalist sides to them. It was the Convention of Royal Burghs which set up the Scottish Development Council in 1932, only one of a range of bodies – the National Trust for Scotland, the Scottish Youth Hostels Association, the Scottish Council for Social Service – which were strongly 'Scottish' in character, culminating with the foundation of the Saltire Society in 1936. By 1939, much of the structure of devolution – represented by the Liberals, by Tom Johnston and by the moderate wing of the SNP under John MacCormick – was in place, beneath the Unionist ascendancy. In the eclipsed SNP the latent issue was, however, this: was Scotland a candidate for dominion status, or for outright, Irish-style independence?

CHAPTER THREE

War, Nationalism and the Covenant

One of the problems we shall certainly have to face is preventing a drift of industry south to England. A few weeks ago Mr Tom Johnston said in the House of Commons that his Department was planning to prevent Scotland suffering the disastrous depression and unemployment which she did after the last war. It is a fact that a certain amount of industrial undertakings have been set up in Scotland since the war began. During the last war the same thing happened; but as soon as the war ended one industry after another closed down. One could mention the closing-down of the dockyards at Invergordon and Rosyth. What guarantee is there that the same thing will not happen after this war – or to a much greater extent? That will be inevitable under an economic system operated by the clique of capitalists. The only solution is the achievement of what the Scottish Peace Front is striving for – the establishment of a Scottish Socialist State, governed by patriotic Scots, solely in the interests and for the welfare of the Scottish nation.

Reichsrundfunk: Radio Caledonia broadcast, intercepted by BBC
Caversham, July 1942

We were now no longer representatives of an old nation in decay, but of a young, virile people lit up with the assurance that whatever men do in unison they can do.

Tom Johnston, 1955

I

The war of 1939–45 was a severe one for Scotland, much more so in retrospect than it seemed at the time. The economy needed to diversify in order to survive; instead war concentrated activity even more on the traditional heavy industries and took a heavy toll of skilled manpower. The Labour Party – after initial flirtation with a very qualified measure of home rule – fixed on centralised planning which had little room for devolution, let alone regional government.

However, it was Scotland's fortune that its most prominent and respected socialist was after 1941 able to preside over a combination of economic experiment and administrative devolution. Tom Johnston, the Red Clydesiders' editor, had turned into a Churchillian patriot, and something more.

Johnston was appointed Secretary of State for Scotland in February 1941. He was already an experienced minister – Churchill had once offered him the Viceroyalty of India – and wise to the ways and means of working the corridors of power. MacDonald had made him junior Scottish Office minister in 1929 and briefly, before being forced into coalition with the Tories in 1931, promoted him to the Cabinet as Lord Privy Seal in charge of unemployment relief schemes. In his *Memories*, Johnston records that the Treasury joked that the demands of the Scottish Office were so persistent that every time they heard he was coming, they would hide the cat's milk.

Labour was divided about the war. Many – Maxton and the Communists – were critical, but Johnston was appalled by the Chamberlain government's attempts at appeasement in the face of the fascist advance in Europe. As war broke out he was serving as Regional Commissioner for Civil Defence in Scotland, in charge of everything from hiding the Scottish Crown Jewels to enforcing the blackout. There was inspiration amid the ghastliness. In the blitz on Clydebank in the spring of 1941, 1500 people were killed and over 50 000 made homeless. And yet the shipyard and factory workers turned up for work day after day and production was barely interrupted.

One incident seems likely to have impressed Churchill. President Roosevelt had sent an envoy, Harry Hopkins, to Britain to assess whether the country was worth supporting with ships and money. Churchill ordered Johnston to join him and Hopkins at a dinner in Glasgow, where Johnston (an amateur genealogist) learned that Hopkins was going to keep quiet about his conclusions. During the meal, Johnston discovered that Hopkins had a grandmother from Auchterarder and mentioned this in a short speech. Replying, Hopkins said he wished to refer to 'the old book to which my grandmother from Auchterarder paid so much attention'. Looking straight at Churchill, he quoted: 'Wheresoever thou goest, we go; and where thou lodgest, we lodge; thy people shall be our people; thy God, our God; even unto the end.' Churchill had the answer he wanted, and American aid was to find in Scotland – in the Clyde, at Scapa, at Prestwick – its key bases.

Churchill summoned Johnston to Downing Street, the latter protesting that at the age of 60 he would rather write history books. Churchill snorted: 'History! Good heavens man, come in here and help me to make history!' But Johnston, despite his bookish protestations, had clearly thought out how he wanted to go about the job. He laid down some conditions. He wanted to try a Council of State for Scotland made up of all the living former Scottish Secretaries, and

Figure 3.1 The Clydebank blitz of 1941.
Photograph provided by Glasgow Museums.
This was one of the most devastating air raids of the war – comparable with the damage the Royal Air Force inflicted on Germany's industrial cities. It emphasised the importance of Scotland to the Allied strategy as the main junction for America-to-Europe supplies, something that gave Johnston powerful leverage.

when they were all agreed on something he would expect Churchill to back it. Churchill promised to 'look sympathetically upon anything about which Scotland is unanimous'.

Johnston's brain overflowed with ideas. An 'industrial parliament' would attract industry northwards and stem emigration; a non profit-making public corporation would use Highland water power for electricity generation; citizenship would be taught in the schools; a sustained drive would improve housing and sanitation and set up a health service; afforestation; and more. Crucially, Johnston was not interested in merely yoking Scotland to the war effort, but in preparing Scotland for an eventual peace. (His Council of State was initially entitled the Council on Post-War Problems.) He thrilled to the possibility that such reforms, 'if we emerged intact as a nation at the end of the war, might mean Scotia resurgent'.

He formed his Council of State (effectively a double-act with Walter Elliot) and it triumphed in 1943 by getting through parliament a bill to set up the North of Scotland Hydro-Electric Board – without a division. A pre-war scheme had been struck down by landed interests and their representatives in the House of Lords, and the mining unions. The Hydro Board started a sequence of programmes to halt Highland economic decline. When an attempt to get the Scots MPs to meet in Edinburgh flopped, he formed an 'industrial parliament'

Figure 3.2
'The greatest Secretary of State'.
Portrait by Sir James Gunn, 1950. Provided by the Scottish National Portrait Gallery.
Tom Johnston, journalist, socialist, home ruler and Secretary of State: 1941–5. As editor of *Forward* in World War I he had been a thorn in Lloyd George's flesh, but the importance of Scotland to the present war effort, particularly after American participation, meant that he was allowed a considerable degree of initiative.

Figure 3.3 Scots girls appeal against being sent south to work in munition factories, 1943.
Photograph provided by *The Herald*.
The conscription of labour, along with factory closures, increased discontent, not only among Nationalists but among Labour MPs. It gave weight to Johnston's programme of administrative devolution and the northward direction of factories.

– the Scottish Council on Industry – drawn from local authorities, chambers of commerce, the Development Council and the Scottish banks. After a phase of deindustrialisation, Johnston estimated that the industrial case it presented helped to establish during the war about 700 businesses employing 90 000 people. It still exists – as the Scottish Council Development and Industry.

The Scottish Office pioneered a scheme which came to be a pilot for the later National Health Service. Pre-war, 'shadow' hospitals were set up to treat casualties which might result from air raids or invasion. Johnston decided that one such well-equipped and well-staffed hospital in Strathclyde should give free examinations and free treatment to civilian war workers. This was extended to all of Scotland and by 1945, the waiting lists for the voluntary hospitals had been cleared. Family doctors were encouraged to use this new service and to send difficult cases to hospital specialists. In a splendid evocation of his Red

Clydeside roots, he turned the 'swagger hotel' at Gleneagles into a fitness centre for coal miners.

II

Johnston had some failures. The teaching of citizenship, an attempt to modernise the curriculum, ran into teacher resistance – although he introduced the idea that domestic science classes should teach nutrition rather than how to bake fancy cakes (but to what effect?). Schoolchildren got free milk, but Johnston didn't get British standard price for milk. (Scottish dairy farmers were disadvantaged by price variations.) But he resisted both the migration of industry production to England, pursued under the Concentration of Industry policy in the name of making production more efficient, and the accumulation of administrative power in London. Instead of Lord Reith's scheme to run town and country planning from a planning ministry in Whitehall, the Scottish Health Department recruited a team which was dedicated to preparing a plan for the Clyde Valley. Instead of the Office of Works becoming Britain's post-war ministry of housing, housing also joined the Health Department's responsibilities, an early example of coordinated government practice.

Four things endured. Scotland's industrial capacity was secured. The country gained a high level of post-war enterprise, although the bias towards heavy manufacturing was to cause problems a decade later.

Second, the 'special case' of the Highlands and Islands was recognised with the Hydro Board; Johnston became its chairman when he retired from politics in 1945. The Board never achieved its objective – to supply enough cheap power to the Highlands to dynamise its industry – but the argument endured, and successive governments have augmented that institutional structure. (Even Mrs Thatcher was prepared to leave the Board in state hands; it was Malcolm Rifkind who insisted on it being privatised.)

Third, the Scottish Office gained additional functions and its success in running them proved that administrative devolution was positively desirable, as in the case of what was, in effect, its national health service. The Ministry of Health in London had, before 1948, the Scottish example to go on. Bureaucratic success played a big part in other wartime policy advances: persuading Whitehall that forestry was a necessary addition to sheep farming in hill areas and that the Forestry Commission should be headquartered in Edinburgh and put under the Scottish Secretary. The momentum of this formidable administrative machine continued even under Johnston's comparatively weak successors, and set the pattern of step-by-step augmentation of responsibility by the Scottish Office in subsequent decades.

Fourth, Johnston's use of political and administrative machinery set a lasting pattern. Although the Scottish Council of Industry and the Council of State might have looked like two different animals from London, in fact they were two arms of the same beast, with the same civil servant as secretary. Johnston's modus operandi was to get the Council of Industry to attack any attempt by the Board of Trade to remove a factory to England, and then to use the political weight of his Council of State to win the day. Their combined strength 'carried guns' and affected north–south politics for decades. When Scottish opinion was mobilised, major concessions could be wrought.

The result was an institutional landscape which accommodated the dominant political vision of the time – that the state should preside over a mixed economy, lead economic development through planning, and shape social development through a welfare state. The Scots' political and administrative machine could now do things in its own way rather than meekly follow London. For example, when the NHS was being formed, the Scottish Office decided that Scotland's teaching hospitals should be part of it, ignoring the embarrassment of the Ministry of Health which wanted to keep London's teaching hospitals out of the NHS.

Johnston created another precedent for later Scottish Secretaries. As Scotland's strongman in the Cabinet he was not above using Whitehall's ignorance of Scotland to imply that if he did not get his way, 'a Sinn Fein movement' would be on its way. This was far from the truth, yet until it ended in the summer of 1942, the Berlin transmitter 'Radio Caledonia' devoted much accurate reporting to Scots discontents, which Johnston relayed ominously to his London colleagues.

The mood of the time was that political will should be mediated through administrative action rather than through democratic forums and 1940s Scotland seemed to have much of the necessary administrative machinery and autonomy. Political debate centred on the extent, not the form, of state power. In this environment, home rule appeared to be an unnecessary abstraction and certainly the divisions in the SNP in wartime provided no secure platform for advancing the cause.

III

In the late 1930s the federalist cause was bubbling away in Britain as a whole, but was riddled with division in Scotland. The right-wing views of Andrew Dewar Gibb, the SNP chairman, were at odds with the leanings of the rest of the leadership. John MacCormick, the secretary, believed that elections were played out; momentum towards home rule would come from all parties supporting a National Convention. Others did not. Divisions persisted over the definition of home rule. Some clung to the idea of dominion status; others were moving towards outright independence.

The war provoked a more disastrous rift. The SNP's pre-war stance was that Scots should play no part in the armed forces unless the government conceded home rule. To MacCormick, this could only damage the party; Scottish opinion supported a just war against fascism. With much difficulty, he persuaded the party that the war against Hitler should be supported, but a strong anti-conscription faction also made leadership concede that moral support should be given to those who refused to be conscripted because of their political beliefs. In these black-or-white times, the SNP's stance of support for the war but not for conscription led to it dithering over contesting a by-election in Tory Argyll in 1940. The SNP eventually put up a candidate, the Glasgow journalist William Power, who won 37 per cent of the vote. The campaign, however, was mainly a critique of the Chamberlain government's conduct of the war and the vote won was a reflection of the government's unpopularity. With the Nazi invasion of Denmark and Norway, and the arrival of Winston Churchill in Downing Street, the SNP moved to wholehearted support of the war effort. Members who supported neutrality were expelled.

Political activity did not cease. MacCormick drummed up support for his National Convention idea, negotiating with the Labour and Liberal parties, and holding the by-election threat in reserve. This met with some success, but MacCormick was being gradually undermined by SNP members who felt that he was not doing enough to voice Scottish grievances and who wanted to sever contacts with 'British' parties. Johnston's consensus (embracing the Tories but not the SNP) negated MacCormick's anti-Tory National Convention.

In 1942, things changed. Douglas Young, a tall, bearded Lallans classicist, was elected chairman of the SNP. Young – actually a Labour Party member – gained kudos for nationalism when he was put on trial for his anti-conscription views; MacCormick's strategy was shredded by a dismal performance in a by-election in Glasgow Cathcart. MacCormick's response was to split the party by walking out and taking a fair number of members with him to concentrate on the Convention plan. Under its new leadership and new secretary, Robert McIntyre, the SNP turned against Labour and Johnston's stewardship. It adopted a socialist rhetoric and a harder pro-independence anti-devolution line, and set about building an organisation, moving away from being a broad-based movement and towards being a more sharply focused political party. It still had its eccentricities, one being urging Scots to eat more cured herrings (but remained outdone by the Secretary of State, with his enthusiasm for smoked mutton instead of bacon and the use of Scottish nettles in papermaking).

Dietary strictures apart, members became convinced that this was the right strategy when Young (about to be jailed) nearly beat Labour in a by-election in Kirkcaldy in 1943. The following year's party conference decided to put forward a social and economic programme for Scotland, not just the simple goal of independence. This was largely formulated by McIntyre and was an interesting if rather eclectic blend of individualism, community and democratic values, and social responsibility. It was soon put to the test in a by-election in Motherwell in April 1945.

McIntyre was the SNP's candidate and, in a straight fight with Labour, captured the seat with 51 per cent of the poll. Labour put this down to the absence of a Tory or a Liberal candidate, and indeed regained the seat at the general

Figure 3.4
Dr Robert McIntyre refuses to take his oath, 1945. Provided by *Punch*. Robert McIntyre wins Motherwell. This was the first SNP victory, after a series of by-elections which showed discontent with the wartime coalition and a wish to avoid the 'betrayal' of 1918. By refusing sponsors, McIntyre caused a minor Commons crisis. 'He is going to be a sad nuisance and pose as martyr,' wrote Sir Harold Nicolson. But two months later, both lost their seats.

McINTYRELEY ALONE
(The Hon. Member for Motherwell)

election just weeks later. But the SNP, ignoring the evidence that the 'party truce' had created a mood for protest voting, thought that Motherwell confirmed the view that the party should seek independence via electoral politics rather than by MacCormick's Convention. McIntyre's speeches in the House of Commons received wide coverage in the press, stressing the value that Westminster could have as a platform for nationalism. From this point on, electoral politics around a left-of-centre platform became central to the party's thinking.

IV

McIntyre's victory was a brief meteor flash across a political firmament which, after the war, reverted rapidly to a struggle between opposing ideologies of left and right. There was no room for other parties, whatever their hue. Scotland also continued to be a corner of a global strategic game which lasted until the early 1990s, and Scottish politics reflected that. Scotland lay on the north-western flank of Europe: essential during the war for supplying the Soviet ally, and thereafter for opposing the Soviet menace. The lochs gave anchorages, first for convoys and later for missile-launching submarines. In a linked sense the involvement of American companies and a generally benign division of UK resources had much to do with keeping the natives contented and remote from the blandishments of Russia, the workers' state to which many Scots, particularly in the trade unions, looked with ingenuous idealism.

After the 1945 election a centralising Labour government had to cope with the problems of the war economy and the export drive which followed it. The national question in Scottish politics was under two influences: a revival in the Labour Party which hadn't been seen since the disaffiliation of the ILP in 1932, and a more conservative, Liberal-dominated agitation towards dominion status. The Labour Party manifesto of 1945 did include a home rule pledge, but this only appeared in the Scottish addition to the British manifesto and was mere window dressing. The party's central belief, shared by much of the population, was that advancing the lot of the working classes required a strong central state. And the idea of dominion status shone less brightly as the sun began to set on the British Empire.

Yet Labour's Scottish Secretaries, Joe Westwood and Arthur Woodburn, were lacklustre, and MacCormick (now moving towards the Liberals) remained convinced that a cross-party movement, bringing in members of the new post-war Scottish establishment like the local authorities and the trade unions, could generate momentum towards home rule. He was encouraged by admissions of support for political devolution wrung from Johnston during various wartime debates. And the fissures in the SNP had, despite McIntyre's brief success, drained it of so much energy (in the 1945 election, it mustered only eight candidates) that there was a political vacuum ready to fill.

MacCormick's Scottish Convention, which had about 1000 members, canvassed all the candidates at the 1945 election about parliamentary support for home rule. More than half replied and only six were hostile. The plans for a National Assembly, shelved in 1939, were dusted off and it was held in 1947 in Glasgow. Perhaps reassured by MacCormick's promise that the Assembly would be a genuine national gathering, about 400 people turned up. All the main political parties sent emissaries, as did the trade unions, local authorities, cultural organisations and the Kirk. Even some businessmen attended, emboldening the Convention to declare this to have been 'the largest and most widely representative meeting ever held in Scotland'.

Three resolutions were debated and one was accepted. It declared the Assembly's conviction that 'a substantial majority of the Scottish people favours a large measure of self-government' and resolved 'to request that the government should forthwith introduce in parliament a bill to give effect to the Scottish self-government proposals'. The Assembly set up a committee which reported to a second Assembly in 1948 on a plan for a parliament with autonomy over domestic affairs and controlling direct taxation. The government, preoccupied with creating the welfare state, paid no attention.

So MacCormick revived another idea – the National Covenant. This unashamedly drew inspiration from the National Covenant drawn up in 1638 in Greyfriars Churchyard, Edinburgh, uniting Presbyterian Scots against the attempts by Charles I to impose his authority on the Kirk. MacCormick worded a declaration calling for a Scottish parliament, but so loosely as to be inoffensive to all parties, and launched it in 1949 at the third meeting of the National Assembly, held in the Assembly Hall of the Church of Scotland and attended by 1200 people. Within a week, it had been signed by 50 000 people and ultimately, it may have been signed by as many as 2.5 million.

This seemed emphatic, but other events showed how weak the fundamental desire was. The Convention was supposed to hold Labour to its home rule manifesto pledge. In 1948, a by-election was held in the Labour stronghold of Paisley. MacCormick believed that as a candidate, he could unite moderate Nationalist, Liberal and Unionist opinion and get in. But the Liberals rejected the idea and although they did not put up a candidate, MacCormick was left looking like a Nationalist horse for Unionist anti-Labour jockeys. To Labour supporters, MacCormick's attacks on London government sounded more like attacks on the Labour government. He lost by 6500 votes and ensured lasting Labour enmity for the Convention and Nationalism.

One spectacular event showed – ultimately – that the fires of Nationalism had burned out. On Christmas Day 1950, MacCormick helped three students

Figure 3.5 The première of *The Three Estates* by Sir David Lindsay (1486–1555) at the Edinburgh Festival in the Assembly Hall in 1948.
Photograph provided by the Scottish Theatre Archive.
Adapted by Robert Kemp and produced by Tyrone Guthrie, this revival after nearly 400 years made Edinburgh jump out of the kailyard and (simultaneously) into the worlds of the Renaissance and Bertolt Brecht. Lindsay's notion of civic morality was to chime in with the ideals of MacCormick's Covenant Movement, but unlike it, the latter, the *Three Estates* lasted. Where the actors strutted, the Scottish Parliament now meets.

steal the Stone of Destiny from underneath the Coronation Throne in Westminster Abbey where it had lain since 1296 when Edward I looted it from Scotland. That this lump of rock, allegedly of biblical origin and certainly the Coronation Stone for Scottish monarchs, had stayed in London despite a promise to return it northwards given by a treaty in 1328, was an affront to all true Nationalists. The escapade certainly generated a vast amount of police activity and an even greater amount of media attention, ending only when the stone reappeared in Arbroath Abbey four months later, but it ignited no political passion. The Tory and Labour parliamentary leaderships, assisted by the discovery of bogus signatures, dismissed the Covenant as irrelevant in a parliamentary democracy. In that arena, there was no Nationalist threat. The SNP could field only three candidates at the 1950 general election (otherwise marked by a Liberal revival that belly-flopped), and only two at the 1951 election, who gained just 12 per cent of the votes cast in the two seats.

MacCormick's agitation succeeded only in persuading the government to

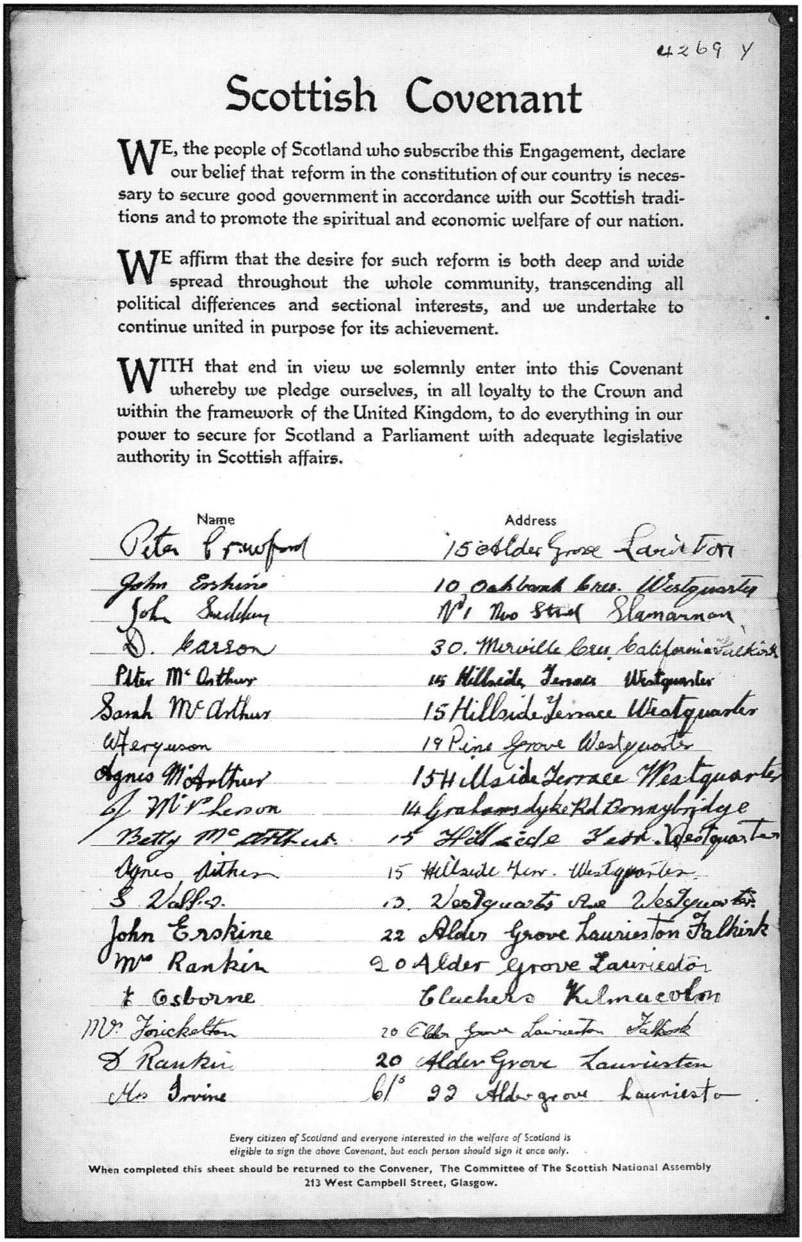

4269 Y

Scottish Covenant

WE, the people of Scotland who subscribe this Engagement, declare our belief that reform in the constitution of our country is necessary to secure good government in accordance with our Scottish traditions and to promote the spiritual and economic welfare of our nation.

WE affirm that the desire for such reform is both deep and wide spread throughout the whole community, transcending all political differences and sectional interests, and we undertake to continue united in purpose for its achievement.

WITH that end in view we solemnly enter into this Covenant whereby we pledge ourselves, in all loyalty to the Crown and within the framework of the United Kingdom, to do everything in our power to secure for Scotland a Parliament with adequate legislative authority in Scottish affairs.

Name	Address
Peter Crawford	15 Alder Grove Laurieston
John Erskine	10 Oakbank Cres. Westquarter
John Suddery	No 1 New Street Slamannan
D. Larson	30. Merville Cres. California Falkirk
Peter McArthur	15 Hillside Terrace Westquarter
Sarah McArthur	15 Hillside Terrace Westquarter
W Ferguson	19 Pine Grove Westquarter
Agnes McArthur	15 Hillside Terrace Westquarter
J McPherson	14 Grahamsdyke Rd Bonnybridge
Betty McArthur	15 Hillside Terr. Westquarter
Agnes Aitken	15 Hillside Terr. Westquarter
S [illegible]	13. Westquarter Ave Westquarter
John Erskine	22 Alder Grove Laurieston Falkirk
Mrs Rankin	20 Alder Grove Laurieston
F Osborne	Clachers Kilmacolm
Mr Frickelton	20 Alder Grove Laurieston Falkirk
S Rankin	20 Alder Grove Laurieston
Mrs Irvine	61/5 92 Alder grove Laurieston

Every citizen of Scotland and everyone interested in the welfare of Scotland is eligible to sign the above Covenant, but each person should sign it once only.

When completed this sheet should be returned to the Convener, The Committee of The Scottish National Assembly 213 West Campbell Street, Glasgow.

Figure 3.6 The Scottish Covenant. Supplied by the Trustees of the National Library of Scotland. A million people had signed the Scottish Covenant (begun in 1949) by mid-1950. Although including the inevitable Roy Rogers and Donald Duck, it was a triumph for its organiser, John MacCormick, who was elected rector of Glasgow University. The Covenant ultimately attracted over 2 million signatures.

Figure 3.7 'The Wee Magic Stane' gets mobile.
Photograph supplied by *The Herald*.
'Kidnapped' from one abbey, Westminster, by associates of John MacCormick on Christmas morning 1950, the 730th anniversary of the Declaration of Arbroath, the Scots Coronation Stone landed up at another, Arbroath, in April 1951. It was sent back to London but not, it turned out, for good.

twiddle with the furniture of centralised government. Woodburn made some slight alteration to parliamentary arrangements for Scottish business, and that was that. He panicked a bit, but nationalism evaporated.

V

The beneficiary of this was not Labour, exhausted after effectively being in power in Scotland for a decade, but the Conservatives who in 1955 briefly reached a majority – though only just – of Scottish seats and 50.1 per cent of the votes. This despite presenting an array of MPs drawn largely from the anglicised upper class and headed by Churchill's confidant James Stuart, an aloof northern laird. Their success reflected the fact that the war had been ambiguous for Scotland. It inflicted severe losses on Scots shipping and on the country's manpower, and the economy that survived was still dominated by the old heavy industries, enlarged to cope with munitions demands. Essentially it was as if World War I and the depression hadn't happened; and the destruction of German and Japanese heavy industrial capacity meant that for over a decade the Scottish economy was closer to its Edwardian apogee than to the miseries of the inter-war period.

But it was a time of minimal investment and technological stagnation. In the

Figure 3.8 'A haaaandbag!': the Queen on her way to inspecting the 'Honours of Scotland' in St Giles' Cathedral, July 1953. Photograph supplied by *The Scotsman*. Professor Gordon Donaldson, though an Episcopalian and a Tory, was distressed at the young Queen's informality when introduced to the Honours of Scotland at St Giles' Cathedral in July 1953. Perhaps he was reconciled when, later, he became Historiographer-Royal, but this was to be only the first of several uncomfortable moments for the House of Windsor and their northern subjects.

shipyards labour relations were terrible, with crazy disputes between unions and a general – and well-justified – suspicion that the bosses of the family firms were keener on repatriating their own profits than in modernising their industries. The Scots-American film director Sandy Mackendrick sketched the type brilliantly – albeit in the context of the Lancashire cotton industry – in Ernest Thesiger as the ancient industrial czar in his brilliant satire *The Man in the White Suit* (1950). His vision of Scotland was equally comic-sinister in *The Maggie* of 1955: the country portrayed as a decrepit coastal puffer, its crew out to loot the credulous, wealthy Yanks.

This stasis was reflected in a generally conservative culture, in which the traditional Scottish institutions were treading water, leaving individuals exposed to a generally unfriendly world. The 1950s have not been much studied, but the impression created by writers like James Kennaway, J. D. Scott, Moray McLaren and Robin Jenkins is of imagination being trapped in a reactionary environment of grey cities, regiments pickled in tradition and a snobbish middle class, flanked by an unthinkingly unionist bourgeoisie and romantic-reactionary nationalists, with 'a chip on the shoulder growing and growing' rather than a cause.

CHAPTER FOUR

The High Tide of Unionism

The principle of centralisation of government in Whitehall and Westminster is emphasised in a manner not hitherto experienced or contemplated in the Act of Union. The supervision, interference and control in the ordinary details of Scottish life and business by the Parliament at Westminster has not hitherto been foreseen, and I frankly admit that it raises new issues between the two nations. . . . I do not therefore wonder that the question of Scottish home rule and all this movement of Scottish nationalism has gained in step with the growth of socialist authority and ambitions in England. I should never adopt the view that Scotland should be forced into the serfdom of socialism as the result of a vote in the House of Commons.

Sir Winston Churchill, 1950

I

As Nationalism – Johnstonian or Covenanting – was spent, Unionism flooded in to occupy the vacant space. Winston Churchill, back in office after the 1951 election, had never been dogmatic about constitutional matters. Way back in 1911, when he was a Liberal MP representing one of the two seats in Dundee, he said:

There is nothing which conflicts with the integrity of the United Kingdom in the setting up of a Scottish Parliament for the discharge of Scottish business. Certainly I am of the opinion that if such a scheme can be brought into existence it will mean a great enrichment not only of the national life of Scotland, but of the politics and public life of the United Kingdom.

He did not voice this opinion in the election campaign, but managed none the less to find some impressive rhetoric which pulled off the singular feat of combining Unionism with small-n nationalism. In a 1950 speech in the Usher Hall, Edinburgh, he voiced the sentiments in the epigraph to this chapter. Was an anti-socialist diatribe a recipe for electoral success? It found plenty of consumers in the 1950s. The Conservatives, still sailing under Unionist colours in Scotland, took seven out of fifteen Glasgow seats in 1950, even working-class Govan. In truth, Churchill needed to do very little to pacify Scottish opinion. The SNP was far less potent a threat than the Communist Party, which kept Willie Gallacher in West Fife until 1955, and had huge influence in the trade unions.

Nevertheless, Churchill did add to the machinery of administrative devolution. He doubled the number of junior Scottish Office ministers to four. In 1953, a Royal Commission chaired by the Earl of Balfour, a landowner and nephew of the languid Edwardian philosopher-premier, was appointed to inquire into the workings of government and the management of the Scottish economy. Although it took some evidence on political devolution, home rule was outwith its remit.

The Commission recognised that there had been a 'general deterioration' in

Figure 4.1 Secretaries of State in the 1980s – Left and Right unionism.
Photograph provided by *The Scotsman*.
Bruce Millan and Willie Ross fraternise with George Younger, Gordon Campbell and John S. Maclay. At the zenith of their power, the Tories were still represented by businessmen and landowners like Maclay, Michael Noble, Campbell and Younger. They had a ready-made network, but this put their more professional colleagues at a disadvantage.

the relationship between Scotland and England. It thought this was due to the government doing both too much to control the economy and too little to decentralise industry to a country which some Scots feared was being treated as a mere province. While this analysis was applauded for its sharpness, the Commission's proposals were derided for their lack of ambition. It advocated shifting responsibility for roads and bridges from the Department of Transport to the Scottish Office but maintained that the Board of Trade's supervision of industrial policy, and therefore the internal UK market, should remain in London. More modestly yet, it thought that the Scottish Secretary should take charge of justices of the peace and animal health.

Defenders of this 'pot-pourri' point out that it did eventually result in the building of the Forth Road Bridge in 1961, and indeed there was no political reason to contemplate anything more radical. In 1955 the Conservatives won, however narrowly, a seat-and-vote majority in Scotland, the only party ever to do so, but from then on the tide turned against them. The root cause was not a failure of domestic imagination but a folly of imperial delusion – Suez.

II

Tory Premier Anthony Eden's attempt to stop Egypt's President Nasser by force from nationalising the Suez canal deeply divided the country, with Scots militarism up against Gladstonian notions of 'international public right'. Young servicemen found themselves drafted out to the canal zone. Students brawled in the Old Quad of Edinburgh University, and the radicals shortly acquired reinforcements when the Communist Party split over the revelations of Stalin's abuses and the Soviet invasion of Hungary.

But Suez's longer-term impact was technological. Prior to Suez, Clyde shipbuilders thought that a 50 000-ton ship was the upper limit for freighters while aircraft were no threat to passenger liners, but the closure of the canal and the necessity to re-route shipping round the Cape of Good Hope created a demand for entirely new types of ship – bulk oil and general carriers of over 100 000 tons. The Clyde yards, restricted in the length of ship they could launch, were unable to supply these superships. This exposed how Scottish industry had failed to invest in technology. Heavy industry in Japan, America and Germany did. Within a decade the great names of Scottish industry were in crisis. Two dozen shipyards in 1950 were reduced to seven in 1968, only two of which made any money. The North British Locomotive Company, which employed 5000 men at Springburn in the second-largest works of its kind in the world in 1950, failed to notice that the railway world was switching from steam to diesel and electric power. By 1963, its workforce was down to 1000. In 1964, it closed.

Nationalists in Scotland were in no position to capitalise on these changes.

They were divided between tactics of contesting elections and other non-parliamentary political means. The veteran campaigner, Roland Muirhead, despite being in his eighties, was sufficiently strongly opposed to electoral politics to leave the SNP and take his pressure group, the Scottish National Congress, with him. This was modelled on India's Congress Party and Muirhead, drawing inspiration from Gandhi, advocated non-violent forms of non-cooperation with the authorities. It achieved nothing. The Scottish Council of the Labour Party, which endorsed home rule in 1947, rejected it completely in 1958. Scotland's future appeared firmly in the hands of Harold Macmillan, who became Prime Minister in 1957.

Macmillan was an extraordinary politician. He carefully cultivated a superior patrician air and worked hard at the art of keeping calm while everything around was collapsing. His premiership was dominated by international affairs, particularly the Cold War and Britain's nuclear deterrence. The only

Figure 4.2 Wendy Wood in action, dancing at a Scottish Patriots' Ball.
Photograph provided by *The Herald*.
Wendy Wood constituted a less toxic version of the *grandes dames* of Irish Nationalism – Maud Gonne, Constance Markiewicz, Julia Comerford – and no demonstration was complete without her green cloak. But in the unionist 1950s this romanticism served to underline the forlornness of the Scottish cause.

Figure 4.3 Harold Macmillan meets pensioners during the Rutherglen by-election, 1962.
Photograph provided by *The Herald*.
Macwonder as magician was already running sour. (The Tories lost the by-election.) Half-American, half-Scots, his superb imitation of a P.G. Wodehouse aristocrat concealed a progressive centrist intellect. He had been Keynes's publisher. He wasn't a home ruler or even particularly pro-Scots (his loyalties were to the North-east of England) but he tried to modernise Scotland, with the help of the STUC and the hindrance of Beeching, Robens, Profumo and so on.

nationalism which bothered him was the 'wind of change' in national consciousness blowing through the continent of Africa. And yet he was not too subsumed by these matters, which required weeks of exhausting travel, to ignore Scottish affairs. The southern tide of affluence which he surfed in the 1959 'you've never had it so good' election did not wash north of the border. To Macmillan 'one-nation' Conservatism really did mean ministering to the whole British nation. Thus this moderate Tory, whose family firm had published the interventionist economic theories of his friend John Maynard Keynes, tried to cultivate a centrist consensus, not far from the pattern of Tom Johnston, in Scotland. With his chief economic adviser, Sir Alec Cairncross, who had edited the standard work on the Scottish economy only a few years before, and his former assistant (and ghost writer) Allan Young, head of the Board of Trade's Scottish office, he developed an alliance with the ex-Communist leader of the STUC, George Middleton. If it did nothing else, it brought together the two most unforgettable faces in the country, Macmillan's bloodhound eyes more than matched by Middleton's appearance, glue from his toupee trickling down the crannies of his Aztec face.

The priority of both men was steel. In 1954, Colville's, now the only major Scottish steel company, decided to spend £20 million on building steel-making blast furnaces at Ravenscraig, near Motherwell. Three years later the Steel Board, which regulated the steel industry after de-nationalisation in 1953, announced that Britain needed a fourth steel strip mill. Both trade union and industrial leaders pressed Scotland's case. With Scottish unemployment almost double (though at 3 per cent) that of England, such a mill would not only provide direct employment, but boost the mining industry and provide the steel necessary for the car production that the industrial lobby hoped to lure to Scotland.

Delegations visited London and Macmillan promised to consider their case sympathetically. After sitting on the decision for over a year, Macmillan eventually announced in 1958 that the new mill would be split, with half going to south Wales and half to Scotland. This, he acknowledged quite plainly, was a political rather than an economic decision as it would create excess production capacity.

This was typical of his unashamedly interventionist industrial policy. The British Motor Corporation opened a vehicle factory at Bathgate in 1961; Wiggins Teape, a paper-making company, was induced to open a pulp mill at Fort William in 1962; and the Rootes Group set up a plant to make Hillman Imp cars at Linwood in 1963; all persuaded by government sticks and carrots. The problem was that this coincided with a drastic rationalisation of other elements of public investment. The Beeching report on the railways in 1961 resulted in the closure of over a third of the system. There were similar shrinkages in the Scottish railway-building industry (which almost vanished), in textiles and in the mines. Where traditional industry survived, this was with a radically reduced workforce, and plenty of resentment was massed against those seen as responsible for their disadvantage. In the 1964 election the Scots took their revenge, voting Labour in the Central Belt and for Liberal candidates in the Highlands.

III

Cue nuclear disarmament. Although Macmillan and his Colonial Secretary Ian MacLeod (both, intriguingly, descended from west coast crofters, in Arran and Lewis respectively) rapidly cleared out of the former colonies, nuclear weapons still conveyed international prestige and drew as much ire from the left. (And not only the left; when Bertrand Russell began his anti-nuclear career with the 'Scientists' Protest' of 1957, the newsreels show him flanked by the craggy features of Lord Boyd Orr and Walter Elliot MP.) The marches from Aldermaston to London started in 1958, and there was from the beginning a strong Scottish contingent, headed by two implacable radicals from (it seemed) the opposite ends of the intellectual spectrum: Hugh MacDiarmid and the Reverend Dr George MacLeod. When Macmillan concluded the Polaris agreement with President Kennedy in 1960 and it was learned that the missile-launching submarines would be based at the Holy Loch, all sections of the Scottish left were mobilised, from Christian pacifists to hard-line Communist trade unionists.

Figure 4.4 Scots disarmers at Aldermaston, Easter 1959.
Photograph provided by Mrs C. MacWhirter.
The anti-nuclear movement united the pacifist, nationalist and socialist traditions – along with skiffle, rock and folk – in a grass-roots movement which Labour found it difficult to cope with.

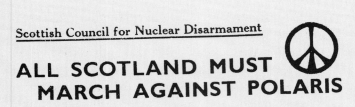

Scottish Council for Nuclear Disarmament

ALL SCOTLAND MUST MARCH AGAINST POLARIS

Saturday 18th February

HON. PRESIDENTS:
THE VERY REV.
DR. GEORGE F. MACLEOD. M.C.
PROF. N. KEMMER, F.R.S

CHAIRMAN:
RODERICK MACFARQUHAR
8 GLENCAIRN CRESCENT
EDINBURGH, 12

SECRETARY:
KENNETH H. MCNEIL
26 KINGSBRAE AVENUE
GLASGOW, S.4
PHONE LAN 2846

SPONSORS:
OLIVER BROWN
DR. ERIC DOTT
PROF. R. W. B. ELLIS
DR. JAMES ROBERTSON JUSTICE
SIR COMPTON MACKENZIE
DR. RONALD MEEK
NAOMI MITCHISON
ALEXANDER MOFFAT
R. E. MUIRHEAD
LORD JOHN BOYD ORR
DR. R. L. M. SYNGE
PROF. C. H. WADDINGTON
DR. ANNE REDPATH
DR. NORA WATTIE

PROTEUS—the Polaris Depot Ship is due in the Holy Loch about February 18th. The George Washington, the first of three submarines arrives in March.

The George Washington Commander, James Osborn, told reporters after her first patrol, that the Polaris missiles with nuclear warheads were "cocked for instant use" throughout the trip.

This stark declaration shows how close the World is to war which could start by human or technical accident or by panic decisions of statesmen or field commanders.

Scotland has been roused by being made a pawn in this conflict that may end in the death of millions of people. Prominent Trade Union leaders, distinguished churchmen, artists, teachers, scientists, engineers, architects and many other people notable in public life have recorded their protest against the folly of the Nuclear Deterrent.

JOIN THE PROTEST

MARCH against POLAR[IS]

SATURDAY, 18th FEBRUARY, 1961 - 2.30

ASSEMBLE AT EYE INFIRMARY, CLAREMONT STREET, GLAS[GOW]

USHER HALL

CANON L. JOHN COLLINS

JUDITH HART, M.P.

Very Rev. Dr. GEO. F. MACLEOD

A. J. P. TAYLOR

Chairman: PROF. N. KEMMER, F.R.S.

POLARIS AND THE PEOPLE

Wed. 14th Dec., 7.30 p.m.
(1960)

ADMISSION 1s.   DOORS OPEN 7 p.m.

EDINBURGH COUNCIL FOR NUCLEAR DISARMAMENT
57 Grange Loan, Edinburgh, 9

THE STANLEY PRESS, EDINBURGH

Figure 4.5
The first CND marches to Holy Loch, 1961.
Poster provided by Chrissie MacWhirter.
Appealing to old Gladstonianism, as well as the new left, the Campaign for Nuclear Disarmament jolted many loyalties in an otherwise rather Conservative decade. The Polaris submarines in the Holy Loch were a particular affront and drew almost annual protests. Labour's backsliding on the issue drove many activists from an ILP background towards Nationalism, including Chrissie MacWhirter, Scottish secretary of CND, who was to become secretary of the SNP in the 1970s.

The anti-nuclear line was defeated by Hugh Gaitskell at the Labour Conference in 1961, but the result was a disaffection within the Scottish left, on which other radical movements could draw. The Campaign for Nuclear Disarmament (CND) was one aspect of a radicalisation in the culture of the period, in drama, poetry and in particular folk-song. Only with the publication of his *Collected Poems* – so called; they were only a fraction of his vast *œuvre* – in 1961 did recognition of Hugh MacDiarmid really break through, along with a new generation of both neo-traditionalists and modernists, from George Mackay Brown and Norman MacCaig to Edwin Morgan and Ian Hamilton Finlay. The folk-song movement, which described an arc from Scotland to the USA of the New Deal and back, provided a language which was secular, socialist and (given the intense suspicion of the Labour establishment)

Figure 4.6 Poets' pub: MacDiarmid, Garioch, MacCaig, Mackay Brown, Bold, Morgan.
Painting by Alexander Moffat. Provided by the Scottish National Portrait Gallery.
It was the literati who kept the national cause alive in the bleak years of the 1950s and early 1960s, but at a certain psychological cost. After a four-hour lunchtime session in Sandy Bell's in Edinburgh Billy Wolfe, leader of the SNP in the 1970s, was heard to remark, 'Sometimes, I feel that the things that will make an independent Scotland worthwhile will be those which prevent us ever getting there.'

Figure 4.7 Hamish Henderson recording folk-singers, 1950.
Photograph provided by the School of Scottish Studies, University of Edinburgh.
Norman Buchan, with Hamish Henderson and Morris Blythman, as Communists, founded the Scottish folk-song movement in the late 1940s, in part as a proletarian alternative to the 'high culture' of the Edinburgh Festival. Their enthusiasm wasn't echoed by Hugh MacDiarmid, but proved very useful in the anti-nuclear agitation of the 1950s and 1960s.

Scottish; it was the second coming of radicals of all sorts, from the Jacobites to John MacLean.

Folk music swelled in the 1960s as an echo of skiffle and the songs of Bob Dylan, Joan Baez and so on. It thrived principally around Aberdeen thanks to the energy of Arthur Argo, a BBC radio producer, and also in and around Glasgow, fuelled by the CND protest movement. Maybe this found a ready audience because people were only too grateful to escape into pub back rooms from Andy Stewart's White Heather Club tartan-and-shortbread museum or the prissy kailyard balladeering of Kenneth McKellar and Moira Anderson which television companies were only too anxious to portray as authentic Scottish culture. This stuff was as kitsch as Sir Walter Scott's royal pageant, which would be realised by anyone confronted with the folk scene. The re-emerging folk music, on the other hand, was underpinned by the scholarly collection of folk songs and music by the likes of Hamish Henderson of Edinburgh University.

To this was added 'reinvented' folk by such pioneers as Archie Fisher, Matt McGinn and Hamish Imlach – rude, bawdy, and radical – a raucous laugh; you took the Battlefield Band with large gulps of beer and whisky. Stuff such as this lured Billy Connolly out of the Clydeside shipyards and into smoky folk dens, out of which he built an international career as an all-round, provided you did not mind the language, entertainer. And it was from the folk club circuit in Fife that Barbara Dickson emerged as a rather more elegant star. Some of this resurgence produced music of outstanding quality, such as the fiddle playing of Aly Bain, which in turn drew the attention of the outside world – for example, Yehudi Menuhin's homages to Shetland fiddle music.

Figure 4.8 Sorley and Sidney in Rose Street.
Photograph provided by Gordon Wright Photo Library.
Sidney Goodsir Smith and Sorley MacLean in the mid-1960s – an urban Joycean and a Raasay Gael. Rose Street was a sort of intellectual junction, not only for Edinburgh's literati but for poets and novelists from a complex cultural landscape. Sidney Goodsir Smith, originally from New Zealand, represented urban bohemia; Sorley MacLean was the greatest Gaelic poet since the eighteenth century.

In the 1960s, under the banners of CND and Anti-Apartheid, Hamish Henderson's lines on John MacLean became an alternative national anthem, and also marked a Scottish involvement in Africa, agitating to break up the Central African Federation; Julius Nyerere in Tanzania and Kenneth Kaunda in Zambia had a Scottish mission-school background, though Kirk elder Hastings Banda in Malawi soon came to seem more like a creation of James Hogg.

This new internationalised left-wing activism found an echo in the media. *The Scotsman* had been bought in 1953 by Roy Thomson, a Canadian press baron, who rescued it from provincial decline. Under the editorship of Alastair Dunnett, one of Johnston's wartime team, who was appointed in 1955, the

Figure 4.9 Sir Alastair Dunnett.
Photograph provided by Lady Dunnett.
As editor, oilman and cultural nationalist, Alastair Dunnett was a formidable figure in gathering publicity and for this he was appointed editor of *The Scotsman* in 1956 by its new Canadian owner, Roy Thomson. Though left-wing, Dunnett had been a press officer for Tom Johnston during the war and was a strong home ruler. His editorship made the once-Unionist *Scotsman* a centre for Lib-Lab schemes of devolution in the late 1950s and 1960s.

newspaper began to rival broadsheet Fleet Street papers. This was especially true of its international news, where *The Scotsman* juggled news agency and its own correspondents' material to produce a first-class foreign news service. Its coverage of African affairs was particularly acute, where the newspaper had a secret edge on competitors – access to the Church of Scotland's network of missionaries. The paper's coverage of the 1950s Mau Mau crisis in Kenya particularly irritated the government, which was trying to pretend that its campaign – itself very violent – to suppress the secret African society was a success. In fact it was not, and as *The Scotsman* reported, murders of Europeans and their African supporters continued. Upset, the Earl of Home, then Foreign Secretary, called in the London editor, Eric Mackay, and his journalist, Neal Ascherson, and pleaded with Mackay 'as a fellow Scot' to tone things down. Mackay replied with a short expletive phrase and left. Scottish radicals continued to enjoy their own brand of news about causes to champion and a place to debate it, an irreverent line which spread to other areas of the media.

The 1960s radicalism powered by Vietnam and rock music, giving youth a voice which the authorities failed to comprehend, reached its zenith in 1968 with riots on campuses in America and on the streets of Paris. But not in Scotland; in fact reactionaries had the best moment when Malcolm Muggeridge preached against students and sin from Knox's pulpit at St Giles, and was promptly followed by the worst hurricane for centuries. When Daniel Cohn-Bendit, one of the leaders of the Paris student protests, was put up for Rector of Glasgow University, the Home Secretary, James Callaghan, refused him entry. Cohn-Bendit lost the election, though in the early 1970s the movement for working student rectors – headed up by one Gordon Brown at Edinburgh – probably got Scottish students more lasting power than anywhere else in Europe.

The theme of 1960s Scotland, instead, was modernisation, foreshadowed by Labour leader Harold Wilson in his 'white heat of technology' speech in 1963. Against this talk, the Tories under the 'instant commoner' Sir Alec Douglas-Home, who became Prime Minister when the Profumo scandal and health problems forced Macmillan to resign in 1963, looked archaic. Sir Alec's vestigial Scottishness did not help his party – they lost seven seats; Labour, with forty-three seats in Scotland, seemed unchallengeably in the ascendant.

CHAPTER FIVE

The Shock of the New

Somewhere among unrhythmic shattering noises of tramways,
Or by cranes and dockyards, steel clanging and slamming,
Somewhere without colour, without beauty, without sunlight,
Among this cautious people, some unhappy and some hungry,
There is a thing being born as it was once born in Florence:
So that a man, fearful, may find his eyes fixed on tomorrow,
And tomorrow is strange for him, aye, full of tearings and breakings,
And to the middle he feels his whole spirit shaken,
But he goes on.

Naomi Mitchison, 'The Scottish Renaissance in Glasgow',
Living Scottish Poets, edited by C. M. Grieve, Ernest Benn, 1931

I

It was 1961 that was actually the year of change: something symbolised materially by the opening of Ravenscraig and the Forth Road Bridge, and the report on the Scottish economy prepared by Sir John Toothill, chairman of Ferranti, for the Scottish Council Development and Industry, perhaps as pregnant for the future as the Whitaker Report had been four years earlier in still-rural Ireland. There were also intellectual stirrings at the Literary Conference at the Edinburgh Festival, with old war-horses of the avant-garde – Henry Miller and William Burroughs – trying to work out just who Hugh MacDiarmid was. MacDiarmid's *Collected Poems* made it into print. So too did *The Democratic Intellect* of his protégé George Davie, a passionate and perceptive statement of intellectual nationalism. Yet the 1960s saw continuity between Macmillan's reforms and those of Labour under Wilson and Willie Ross, his Scottish Secretary. The object was rather the same as that of the planning movement in the 1930s: to produce a more balanced 'mix' of industry, favouring consumer goods over capital goods and trying to raise general living standards to foster new markets. The old Scotland of cramped housing and grim town centres, inadequate roads and hierarchical, tawse-governed education became an immediate target.

Wilson was an economist and his mission was to revive the British economy.

Figure 5.1 Ravenscraig Steelworks opens, 1961.
Photograph provided by *The Herald*.
Should it ever have been built? Colville's had wanted a riverside steelworks at Erskine; the steel industry wanted a single strip mill in Wales. Harold Macmillan's compromise was dependent on the success of the new Scottish motor industry. When Linwood and Bathgate closed as a result of the soaring petrol-pound in the early 1980s, it was doomed.

Distrustful of the Treasury, he charged a new Whitehall ministry – the Department of Economic Affairs under George Brown as deputy Prime Minister – to come up with a national economic plan for recovery. The Scottish Office sprouted the Scottish Development Department which recruited economists and planners. Ross equipped himself with a Scottish Economic Planning Council composed of industrialists, bankers, trade unionists and local councillors. Economic planning was able to proceed apace because the civil servants already had Toothill to hand. Ross plunged into a blizzard of activity. The Highlands and Islands Development Board was set up in 1965. The drive to bring in comprehensive education was begun, as was the reform of social work,

Figure 5.2
Willie Ross and
the Brave New
World, 1968.
Photograph
provided by *The
Herald*.
The Secretary of
State and the Lord
Provost of
Glasgow up
against an
achievement of
the 1964–70
government that
many subsequently
worried about:
a multi-storey
Glasgow housing
block. The
upheavals involved
in this huge social
experiment
probably had a
role in shaking
loose old political
loyalties.

particularly the treatment of wayward children. George Brown's department weighed in to rescue Fairfield's shipyard on the Clyde. Public spending, particularly on new council housing, was increased. The government's plan for Scotland ambitiously envisaged an end to emigration, unemployment and low wages through the direction of industries and subsidies, which were to be available everywhere in Scotland except in Edinburgh and Leith. A new electronics industry was to be built. In the 1966 election, the Scots approved. Labour took 49.9 per cent of the vote and three more seats.

By the end of the decade much of Scotland would, through a construction boom, have become unrecognisable. Hundreds of thousands of houses – mostly inadequate, but including some innocent bystanders – were flattened in favour of tower blocks. Schools and training colleges were assembled almost from kits, motorways and dual carriageways were ramified, and car ownership began its steeply upward ascent. More resources were aimed at physical and social planning and higher educational reform. The latter included the 'new' universities of Stirling, Strathclyde and Dundee, and in 1969 the formation of an

Figure 5.3 Wilson and Reith.
Photograph provided by *The Herald*.
Harold Wilson with High Commissioner Lord Reith at the General Assembly of the Kirk in 1966: a former white-heat man dimmed to a glow and an extinct volcano of Scoto-Britishness.

all-British hi-tech institution which had through its planners, Jennie Lee and Walter Perry, a strong Scottish pedigree: the Open University.

Unfortunately – though alas symbolically – the new Highlands and Islands Development Board built for itself two hideous office blocks which disfigured the waterfront of Inverness. Modernisation came unapologetically and raw, through comprehensive redevelopment plans and motorways blasting through central Glasgow, despite the creation of bipartisan planning bodies. Robin Cook, then a young councillor in Edinburgh, said his Glasgow opposite number Tom Fulton had a positive mission to destroy every historic building in the city. But Edinburgh wasn't far behind, with the demolition of nearly every decent building on Princes Street and – thanks to the University – most of George Square. Not only did rail closures isolate the Borders and the North-east; the Forth and Clyde Canal was closed in 1962, on the eve of a boom in leisure sailing, while most of the Clyde steamers were scrapped.

'There's an auld hoose, ding it doon!' commented the nationalist actor – and pioneer foodie and conservationist – Moultrie Kelsall. Opposing all of this indirectly was a politicising process. Although Scotland was treated as a separate planning unit, the ethos of these schemes was British: an attempt to revive central planning. But it was a Britishness which, though taken for granted after World War II, was in fact on the wane. Already the first moves of the establishment mind towards Europe were visible, as was the deterioration in notions of 'British homogeneity'. This meant that electoral reactions, after briefly favouring the Conservatives, took on a specifically Scottish identity.

II

Hopes were high, and yet within weeks of the 1966 election, things went horribly wrong for Harold Wilson. Faced with worse than expected economic and financial forecasts, his government needed to raise taxes. It introduced the Selective Employment Tax which was intended to encourage manufacturing industry at the expense of service firms but was, in effect, a tax on jobs. The seamen went on strike, weakening sterling and pushing the government into deflationary measures and curbs on trade unions. Interest rates rose and a wages freeze was announced. Unemployment in Scotland started to climb sharply. Hitting Labour's activists where it hurt were Wilson's support of the US in Vietnam, his overtures to Europe, and continuing nuclear rearmament.

Dashed hopes and feelings of betrayal were, not for the last time, a fertile breeding ground for the SNP. The party had already begun to recover in the early 1960s. In 1962, a by-election was held in West Lothian. The SNP's chosen candidate was a recent recruit – Billy Wolfe. He lived locally, was a chartered accountant and worked in his family's manufacturing firm, but he was also a nuclear disarmer, industrial cooperator and, given the chance, something of a poetic mystic. Labour's choice was an odd one, an old Etonian local laird, Tam Dalyell, whose current preoccupation (and Dalyell had probably the most merciless one-track mind in British politics) was ship schools. Wolfe's campaign concentrated on the demise of the local shale oil industry which had once employed 12 000 people. Since the government had just removed a subsidy to the industry, it was easy enough to blame London mismanagement. His campaign slogan was 'Put Scotland First'. Dalyell won comfortably enough with 21 266 votes, but Wolfe came second with 9750. In the 1964 election Wolfe pushed his vote up to 15 087 and still higher to 17 955 in the 1966 election.

These campaigns helped push Wolfe to prominence. He became an executive vice-chairman of the party. People attracted to the SNP by Wolfe's campaigning

Figure 5.4 William Wolfe revives the SNP in West Lothian, 1962.
Photograph provided by Gordon Wright Photo Library.
In the aftermath of the closure of the Scottish shale oil industry, William Wolfe, a local industrialist and accountant, ran second to the Labour candidate, Tam Dalyell, descendant of 'Black Tam o' the Binns', scourge of the Covenanters. His innovations in policy and publicity were to help make the SNP a formidable force within a few years.

included a Linlithgow teenager, Alex Salmond. More importantly in the short term, Ian MacDonald, an Ayrshire farmer, decided to give up farming and work as a full-time organiser. Between 1962 and 1968, under the banner of the stylised SNP thistle, the number of party branches rocketed from 20 to 484. Claims of a membership of 120 000 were made, but these were a gross exaggeration. Nevertheless, the SNP was becoming a serious campaigning party. It fought fifteen seats in 1964 and twenty-three two years later, gaining 14 per cent of the votes cast in the seats contested.

With this momentum and against a darkening economic background, hindsight says that an eventual SNP breakthrough ought to have been obvious. But it was not, even though a by-election in Glasgow Pollok in early 1967 produced a real shock. The SNP had never contested the seat before but George Leslie, a vet, came from nowhere to take 28 per cent of the vote. He took some votes from the Conservatives but a lot more from Labour, enabling the Tory, Esmond Wright, a history professor and BBC political commentator, to win the seat. It was to be the last seat that the Scottish Tories took at a by-election from another party in the twentieth century. The Liberals were humiliated. Smarting, they rejected overtures from the SNP to form a pro-home rule pact. One prominent Liberal supporter of this idea, Ludovic Kennedy, promptly quit and joined the SNP.

The bandwagon carried on rolling in May's local elections. The SNP gained a fair smattering of seats and the prize of being the largest party in Stirling. Robert McIntyre, the ex-MP, became the town's provost. The Nationalists pitched into anti-EEC campaigning as the Labour government started Common Market entry negotiations. Their demand for a referendum helped keep them in the public eye. And in October, Willie Ross decided that Tom Fraser, the elderly Labour MP for Hamilton, should be appointed chairman of the Hydro Board.

From the start, the SNP relished the campaign. It was a seat the Nationalists had fought before and they had been quietly preparing for a by-election on the basis of rumours that Fraser was in line for a peerage. And from the start, Labour fumbled. The National Union of Mineworkers insisted its candidate, Alex Wilson, had to be chosen, to the disgust of many Labour members. (Only a couple of mines were left in the once-mighty Lanarkshire coalfield.) The SNP picked Winnie Ewing, a young, articulate Glasgow lawyer. Televison cameras and photographers' lenses gobbled her up; Wilson proved indigestible. Labour's massive majority melted away in the face of Ewing's charm, grim economic reality (sterling was in full flight and devaluation was just days away) and the efforts of hundreds of SNP members from all over the country.

The figures do not matter. The SNP victory did. The reaction was electrifying. People queued outside party offices to join. Officials were overwhelmed with

Figure 5.5 Winnie Ewing wins the Hamilton by-election, November 1967.
Photograph provided by *The Herald*.
This was one of Labour's self-made disasters. The National Union of Mineworkers got its man selected; the local party was aggrieved; the SNP had an articulate and photogenic candidate. Then Harold Wilson was faced with a sterling crisis. After two decades of stasis the SNP was on its way.

media demands for interviews, information, photographs. A train was hired to take Ewing and hundreds of supporters to Westminster in triumph. She arrived at parliament's doors, not in a black limousine but a red Scottish-made Hillman Imp. Within a few weeks, Ewing generated more publicity than the SNP had had, Wolfe reckoned, in the previous twenty years.

Hindsight also says that the collapsing economy was only part of the reason for the Nationalist success. The SNP could also draw on the hammerblows which the transformation of the 1960s inflicted on traditional Scottish society. The 1960s had their own ethos – youth fashion, sexual permissiveness, a new hedonism – but in fact the Britain of the beginning of the decade was far closer to the 1900s. Contraception, mass motorisation, plastics, air transport were unknown to the mass of the people; by the end of the decade these had become commonplace. Despite the modernising pretensions of the government, there was no real understanding of this upheaval until 1968, and by then it was too late to do much about it.

This meant that reforms such as those in local government and housing produced a demand for security in other directions, which the institutions of civil society simply couldn't cope with. While this change was limited – it still didn't affect well-unionised workers or the traditional middle class – the 'displaced' sought security, however temporary, in the inspirational politics of Nationalism. The pattern of local election results in 1968, when the SNP took a staggering 34 per cent of the vote, showed that the Nationalists were doing best in the new towns full of people decanted from familiar tenemented streets and industrial labour into unfamiliar avenues and jobs, such as in Cumbernauld where they took control.

III

The Conservatives were fastest to react to Hamilton. After the 1966 defeat, something of an intellectual revival took place. Aspirant MPs such as Michael Ancram, Malcolm Rifkind, Peter Fraser and Alex Fletcher formed the Thistle Group, aiming to reassert a Scottish Tory identity. Glasgow Cathcart MP Teddy Taylor gave a working-class counterbalance to the grouse moor image. (Michael Ancram hid rather than flaunted his aristocratic background.) The party set up a committee under Sir William McEwan Younger (of the brewing dynasty) to look at how the system of government in Scotland might be improved.

After the fillip of Pollok and the shock of Hamilton, the Tories realised their own votes were as much under threat as Labour's. In the aftermath, both the McEwan Younger committee and the Thistle Group published reports arguing that bureaucracy was smothering Scotland. In 1937, two Scottish Office ministers supervised 2400 civil servants. By 1970, this had swelled to six ministers and 8300 civil servants. The great planning solutions embarked on with such utopian hope were now decaying corpses. There was no hope of finding the money to implement them. A damning report published in 1967 declared that one in three Scots lived in houses which were either substandard or unfit. The solution, the Tories thought, was not to slash the bureaucracy but to exert more political control over it. 'We are convinced that a measure of devolution over Scotland's domestic affairs is essential,' wrote the Thistle Group.

This encouraged Edward Heath, the Tory leader, to go to the Scottish Tory conference in Perth in 1968 with a startling proposal which was pretty much his own idea. Heath opened his speech by dwelling on national traditions, not British national traditions but Scottish national traditions. His audience sat up. Surely Ted was not turning into a Nat? No, he abjured independence as being

Figure 5.6 Edward Heath in Scotland, 1965.
Photograph provided by *The Herald*.
Pictured after being elected leader of the Conservative Party in 1965, with two of the party's grandees, Michael Noble (Secretary of State 1962–4) and Sir Hugh Fraser, the astute Glasgow businessman who became, by a succession of spectacular takeovers, owner of Harrods. With such powerful backers Heath thought that a Tory revival in Scotland was still a possibility, hence his enthusiasm for a qualified measure of devolution, but even in his victory year, 1970, the Tory vote scarcely increased to 38 per cent. By his last election, October 1974, it was down to 24.7 per cent, less than half its 1955 level.

against the trend of integration in Europe. The audience relaxed. But then he stirred them, pointing out that devolved government in Northern Ireland had many advantages. And then he hit them: 'We would propose . . . the creation of an elected Scottish Assembly, to sit in Scotland. What we have in mind is that this Scottish Assembly would be a single chamber, and would take part in legislation in conjunction with Parliament.' This the press dubbed Heath's 'Declaration of Perth'. There were, he admitted, a lot of unanswered questions as to what this Assembly would do. So he set up a committee under the chairmanship of Sir Alec Douglas-Home to draw up a plan. The Tories were as

Figure 5.7
Bannockburn,
1968.
Photograph
provided by
Gordon Wright
Photo Library.
Pilkington-
Jackson's huge
statue of the
Bruce, surveyed
by kids trying to
work out why
it's there.

astonished as if Heath had changed out of a suit and into a kilt in full public view.

In effect, Heath was trying to repeat the unionism/nationalism combination trick worked by Churchill in 1951 with the added knob of a firm policy proposal. No one explained this to the party, however, many of whom thought their leader just sounded like a nationalist. Stunned into silence, the dissidents recovered their voices when Sir Alec reported back in May 1970. His plan for a 125-member elected Scottish Convention which would handle intermediate stages of Scottish legislation was accepted, but only after critics accused him and Heath of undermining the Union, so persuading a quarter of the conference to vote against the proposals. In a party where loyalty to the leadership is the gold standard, this was shocking stuff.

IV

The government and the Scottish Labour Party were meantime struggling to cope with the Nationalist threat. Willie Ross was in no doubt as to what should be done. At the 1968 Scottish party conference, he fulminated against the 'tartan Tory' Nationalists who should be attacked head-on and defeated. The rest of the government was not so sure. Richard Crossman, Lord President of the Council, believed legislative devolution was needed. The outcome of the 1968

Figure 5.8 Home rule in the 1960s.
Photograph provided by Gordon Wright Photo Library.
Ferry Road, Edinburgh. Graffiti was in its infancy: a derelict railway bridge over a bypass near a bleak scheme on the outskirts of Edinburgh. It was from this unvisited Scotland, far from Rose Street, that the first wave of nationalist revival was to come.

Figure 5.9 A 1320 club symposium, 1968.
Photograph provided by Gordon Wright Photo Library.
The 1320 Club was an attempt by Hugh MacDiarmid, Oliver Brown (centre) and other nationalist gadflies to inject a bit of intellect into the nationalist revival of the 1960s. They got the length of symposia featuring the likes of Harry Hanham, the New Zealander political scientist whose *Scottish Nationalism* (1968) was a pioneer effort, Prof. Gavin McCrone and even Nicky Fairbairn, before succumbing to the fundamentalism of Ronald MacDonald Douglas (second from right).

conference, where pro-devolution motions were roundly defeated, half-convinced Wilson that Ross was right, but Crossman continued to agitate and managed to get a ministerial devolution committee set up. This limited itself to recommending procedural and administrative changes, resulting in an investigatorial parliamentary select committee on Scottish affairs being set up in 1968. But Crossman, who seems to have resented Ross for keeping Scottish affairs privy from English MPs, did not give up and suggested to Wilson that setting up a Royal Commission on devolution would be a good idea. Ross reluctantly agreed, supposing that at least it would kick the issue into the long grass from where it might never return. The Scottish Labour Party's own conclusions, reached after a committee discussed it for two years, were that a devolved assembly would be dangerously divisive. Its evidence to the Royal Commission, initially chaired by Lord Crowther when it was set up in 1969, was to reject devolution. John Mackintosh, East Lothian's Labour MP, historian of the British Cabinet, political maverick and legendary raver, put himself even farther beyond the pale by fighting hard for self-government.

Rather oddly, despite this evidence that the SNP upsurge was forcing the two main parties to pay a lot of attention to Scotland, the Nationalist fire seemed to die down as fast as it had flared up. SNP councillors who found themselves in office, not in power, were made to pay for their inexperience. Only a minority survived in politics. A curious episode shortly after Hamilton illustrated the party's opportunism rather than principle. The Argyll and Sutherland Highlanders returned to their barracks in Stirling soon after fighting a fierce and nasty little battle in Aden, a British colony, against Arab insurgents. The assault, led by Lieutenant-Colonel Colin Mitchell, was courageous and thus

Figure 5.10 'Mad Mitch' is presented with the Freedom of Stirling, 1968.
Photograph provided by *The Herald*.
Lt-Col Colin Mitchell's clearing out of Arab nationalists from Aden was a piece of derring-do but at the wrong end of empire. The subsequent disbandment of the Argyll and Sutherland Highlanders seemed to be the revenge of military bureaucrats in Whitehall. Robert McIntyre, as Provost, presented him with the Freedom of Stirling, confirming left-wing suspicion of the Nationalists as 'tartan Tories'. Yet when Mitchell went into politics it was as a Conservative. He was elected for West Aberdeenshire in 1970 but, after a short and unhappy career, left the House in 1974.

conformed to the traditional image of the Scottish warrior. But 'Mad' Mitch, as he became better known, could also be seen as an imperial relic, unwanted in a modern Scotland. Nevertheless Provost Robert McIntyre gave Mitchell a hero's welcome, particularly since the government had just announced it was to disband Mitchell's regiment. This unexpected glorification of militarism was repugnant to radical Nationalists who saw Scotland as England's last colony, not least because of persistent stories that Mitchell was about to become an SNP parliamentary candidate. He did indeed stand for parliament in the 1970 election, but for the Tories, winning West Aberdeenshire which he served for four undistinguished years. Some other young SNPers – including George Robertson and Brian Wilson – migrated to Labour and condemned nationalism in every shape and form.

The lack of a coherent set of policies in local government led the party into trouble. Its vote fell sharply in the May 1969 local elections. In a parliamentary

Figure 5.11 and 5.12 (above and opposite) A demonstration against the Bloody Sunday shootings and one against the IRA staged by the Orange Order, both in 1969.
Photographs provided by *The Herald*.
These two photographs show why the Scots, including Catholic Scots, treated Irish issues with great delicacy. Although sympathisers with Sinn Fein and Orangemen were minorities within their own confessions, the latter were potentially a mass force.

by-election in Glasgow Gorbals, the SNP encountered Labour's bedrock Catholic support (Labour's posters were printed in green) and could not shift it. When the death of Emrys Hughes, son-in-law of Keir Hardie, former *Forward* editor and home ruler (he scunnered the party by sponsoring Winnie Ewing when she took her seat), caused a by-election in the socialist heartland of South Ayrshire, where Orangeism is more to the fore, Labour was equally impregnable. An unyielding unionist campaign sent Jim Sillars to join Labour's ranks in the Commons. And only a few miles west of Stranraer, 'old, unhappy far-off things, and battles long ago' turned out, with the beginnings of the Ulster troubles, not to be old or far off at all.

In the 1970 election, the boost to membership and money caused by Hamilton enabled the SNP to field sixty-five candidates and to double its share of the Scottish vote to 11.4 per cent. But in terms of votes per candidate, the result was actually a slip back from 1966. Ewing lost her seat, and the SNP's capture of the Western Isles by Donald Stewart, Stornoway's provost, was little consolation. Instead, the big surprise of the election was a British one. Against the predictions of the polls, Harold Wilson lost and the Tories under Edward Heath were back, gaining three Scottish seats. Now the constitutional genie was out of the bottle. The Royal Commission would continue to roll, devolution was still a live issue, and the wholly unexpected discovery of untold wealth under the North Sea would alter the debate again.

CHAPTER SIX

Oiling the Slippery Slope

When you see the Queen in action, everything is just absorbed into this frozen feudal hierarchy. All the old bigwigs are brought out into the open as if they were somehow responsible for a great industrial achievement, while the workers are presented as natives and barbarians who can be greeted but have to be kept at a distance . . . this great Scottish occasion was just an opportunity for the London establishment to come up and lord it over the Scots.

Tony Benn, *Diaries*, 3 November 1975

Syne the rose shrivelled suddenly
As a balloon is burst,
The thistle was a ghaistly stick
As gin it had been curst.

Was it the ancient vicious sway
Imposed itsel' again,
Or nerve owre weak for new emprise
That made the effort vain,
A coward strain in that lorn growth
That wrocht the sorry trick?
The thistle like a rocket soared
And cam doon like the stick.

Hugh MacDiarmid,
'A Drunk Man Looks at the Thistle'

I

Oil and devolution impacted on all political institutions, but particularly on a political class which was unused to the sort of prominence that it now achieved. Hitherto only the Scottish Secretary or the (few) high-flying Westminster Scots, like Sir Alec Douglas-Home, got much public recognition in Scotland. But oil was to propel such Nationalists as Gordon Wilson, George Reid and Margaret Bain (now Ewing) to prominence, and devolution did the same for back-bench Labour MPs such as John Smith, Jim Sillars, Robin Cook

Figure 6.1
Alexander
Frederick
Douglas-Home,
Lord Home of the
Hirsel,10 March
1988.
Oil on canvas,
90.8 x 70.2 cm.
Provided by the
Scottish National
Portrait Gallery.
© Avigdor Arikha,
courtesy,
Marlborough
Gallery, New
York.
In 1979 Lord
Home dropped a
bombshell on the
'yes' side by
advising Scots to
'Vote NO for
something
better!' –
interpreted as
being a
parliament with
taxation powers.
The notion was
that his party
would deliver on
this. Some hope.

and Tam Dalyell, Tories such as Malcolm Rifkind, Teddy Taylor and Alick Buchanan-Smith, and Liberals such as Russell Johnston and David Steel. Scotland had yet to secure a parliament, but in the 1970s it gained a political élite.

BP had hit gas in 1965, off East Anglia. A minor oil field was found in Danish waters in 1967, but it wasn't until Phillips discovered the big Ekofisk field in Norwegian waters in 1969 that interest began to mount. Even so, in 1970 after five years of exploration, Sir Eric Drake, chairman of BP, told reporters: 'There won't be a major field there.' Six months later, BP announced it had found the giant Forties oilfield which, by 1977, was producing 500 000 barrels of oil a day, equivalent to a quarter of Nigeria's entire daily production. Even so, there was still no goldrush fever. In the early 1970s, companies reckoned their exploration costs were about $15 million per oil strike and then getting the stuff out to a refinery could cost anything between $50 and $150 million. With crude oil prices bumping along at $4–5 a barrel only big fields looked profitable. That all changed in 1973 when crises in the Middle East and action to force prices up by the Organisation of Petroleum Exporting Countries' cartel sent prices rocketing to $14–16 a barrel. Suddenly, small oilfields looked likely to yield big profits and Britain seemed to be sitting on a goldmine.

But whose goldmine? The SNP were fast off the mark. Noting that most, if not all of the British oil finds were off Scotland's coast, Gordon Wilson,

Figure 6.2
The SNP launches the 'It's Scotland's oil!' campaign, 1972. Photograph provided by the SNP. There was a point in 1973–4 when the SNP's Gordon Wilson and Donald Bain knew more about oil than Her Majesty's Government. The issue became critical when the price of oil staged a fourfold increase in the autumn of 1973 as a result of Arab action during the Yom Kippur war.

Dundee lawyer and SNP vice-chairman, industrious though short on charisma, began a campaign to get oil tax revenues put into a special fund and spent in Scotland, which is what the Norwegians had decided to do. But no one knew what the revenues would be, or what oil meant in terms of jobs. The North-east of Scotland Development Agency guessed at 2000 jobs in Aberdeen, but economists at Aberdeen University scoffed, suggesting that only the Moray Firth area might benefit from oil platform construction work. But increasingly the SNP's bullish forecasts, immediately pooh-poohed by the government, were proved correct as find after find was announced. Did the SNP know more about North Sea oil than the government? It did; petroleum policy was a farce. Was the SNP saying that if Scotland controlled the oil, Scots would be rich? It was.

It was a timely idea, for heavy manufacturing industry, the soul of the Scottish economy, was in deep trouble. To help the Clyde shipyards meet competition from East Asian shipbuilders, the yards had been reorganised into two consortia. In 1971, Heath's government refused to grant further subsidy to the four yards in Upper Clyde Shipbuilders (UCS), which then went into liquidation. (Sir Eric Yarrow had bought the shares in the fifth, Yarrow's.) On the line weren't just the jobs of the 8500 shipyard workers, but many more in steel, transport and mining. The shop stewards – Jimmy Reid and Jimmy Airlie, both Communists – conjured up the spirit of the Clyde Workers' Committee, but eschewed strike action and went for the novel idea of conducting a work-in to complete the yards' £90 million contracts. In a famous speech, Reid told the workers: 'We will conduct ourselves with dignity. There will be no bevvying,' an alcohol abstinence line which passed into trade union folklore as the Clydeside motion.

The work-in caught the public imagination, not just in Scotland but around the world. John Lennon and Yoko Ono were among thousands who sent donations. In Scotland, Labour and Nationalist politicians, churchmen, journalists and actors rallied to the cause. In September 70 000 marched. A 48-hour strike by other workers brought out 100 000. Seven months after the UCS occupation began, the government caved in, offering £35 million to keep three of the yards working and a £12 million dowry to an oil rig construction firm to take over the fourth.

The political consequences were immense. The government's industrial strategy, which had been hitherto based on slaughtering 'lame ducks', was in tatters. Trade union and workers' solidarity had won a major victory, terminally eroding a once-substantial Tory working-class vote in Glasgow. The illusion that workers could hold the keys to an industrial heaven was rudely shattered in 1975 when the *Scottish Daily News*, a workers' cooperative-based daily newspaper born out of the withdrawal of Express Newspapers from production in Scotland,

Figure 6.3 The Upper Clyde Shipbuilders crisis, autumn 1971.
Photograph provided by *The Herald*.
Hugh Scanlan, Jimmie Airlie, Tony Benn, Jimmie Reid and Willie Ross lead a protest march through Glasgow during the threat to close down shipbuilding on the Upper Clyde. What seemed like a dawning of the Red Clyde proved ultimately another stage in a grim battle for survival.

collapsed under the autocratic direction of Robert Maxwell, brought in to rescue the paper from internal bickering. Yet the SNP asserted that with independence, proud Scots would not need to go cap-in-hand to London; oil revenues would allow them to stand on their own two feet. Jimmy Reid was derisive of the SNP, saying that they were promising four taps in every Scottish household – one for cold water, one for hot water, one for oil and one for whisky – but he still sounded more Scots than Communist.

II

Yet opinion polls, now being conducted with increasing frequency, suggested that people were listening to the SNP. In 1971, the Nationalists first used the oil issue in a parliamentary by-election in Falkirk, Stirling and Grangemouth burghs. The veteran Robert McIntyre won a third of the vote, giving Labour a bit of a fright. On the back of the UCS work-in, the Scottish Trades Union Congress held a meeting billed as a 'Scottish Assembly' in Edinburgh. About 1500 people turned up, not just trade unionists, but representatives from all political parties, local authorities, business, churches and so on. The purpose was to seek a common economic strategy to deal with Scotland's unemployment strategy, but what emerged was a surprisingly strong home rule sentiment. So strong indeed, that the representative of the Confederation of British Industry (CBI) agreed to go away and rethink his scepticism about devolution.

Devolution had moved from the arcane fringes of politics to become a pre-occupation. The Royal Commission, now chaired by Lord Kilbrandon after the death of Lord Crowther, was busy taking evidence and publishing research papers, giving the subject an establishment respectability. In September 1972, the SNP upped the ante, beginning the 'It's Scotland's Oil' campaign, posters which were followed by a 'Rich Scots or Poor British?' series. Accusations of anti-English selfishness poured in on the SNP, but the opinion polls suggested that a good many Scots seemed to think that the Nationalists had a point.

In early 1973, Gordon Wilson, the mastermind of the oil campaign, was picked as the SNP candidate in a parliamentary by-election in his home constituency, Labour-held Dundee East. Wilson more than trebled the Nationalist share of the vote and came within an ace of winning. Labour's choice of candidate seemed to symbolise the miserable state into which many Scots felt their country had fallen. To replace George Thomson, a popular and able Dundonian who had been appointed as a European commissioner, Labour chose George Machin, a dull trade unionist from Yorkshire who knew little about Scotland and even less about Dundee.

In truth, the Scots had plenty of reasons to think that Scotland had become the plaything of other people, especially rich, uncaring people, and was at the mercy of powerful foreign forces. In the Highlands, fury was aroused by the actions of several estate owners who seemed to think that the land they owned was their personal kingdom to do with as they liked, regardless of the effect their actions, or more usually inaction, had on the people who lived there. Typical was Dr John Green, who lived in Sussex and bought much of the island of Raasay, off Skye, for less than £10 000. 'The Howard Hughes of the Hebrides' never visited his purchase, and allowed the Raasay House Hotel and other properties to go to rack and ruin. He turned a deaf ear to the islanders' plea to sell one-fifth of an acre for a car ferry slipway. Green's neglect received wide publicity in the Scottish media, as did that of others.

The oil industry proved not to be an unmitigated boon either. British companies did not have the resources for the fast exploitation of the new wealth which the government wanted, so the door was wide open to big American

Figure 6.4 An SNP Bannockburn Day commemoration.
Photograph provided by Gordon Wright Photo Library.
Though political nationalism marked time, 'small-n' nationalism commemorated Bruce's victory at Bannockburn, subsequently a field of pilgrimage for the SNP. Here, Gordon Wilson addresses a rally.

firms. Scottish companies did not have the capacity or the expertise to supply these firms, so they bought what they needed from their usual, American, suppliers. This caused immense social strain, ranging from locals being priced out of housing markets to outrage at the government's apparent willingness to let the oil firms do pretty much what they wanted – such as building an oil refinery on the outstandingly beautiful Cromarty Firth, a plan which never materialised more by good fortune than by design. Sure, plenty of Scots became unexpectedly rich from oil, but plenty more became bewildered victims of change.

This injustice, the upheaval and the backlash against both, was brilliantly captured in John McGrath's play *The Cheviot, the Stag and the Black, Black Oil*. This Marxist polemic, tracing the ills of the Highlands from eighteenth-century evictions to twentieth-century desecrations and ascribing them to the monopoly ownership of land and capital, played to packed and ecstatic houses wherever McGrath took his 7:84 company (named after a contemporary statistic that 7 per cent of the people owned 84 per cent of the wealth). Although McGrath

Figure 6.5
The Cheviot, the Stag and the Black, Black Oil: John McGrath and his troupe stir things up in the glens. Photograph provided by the Scottish Theatre Archive. The magazine *Scottish International* was something of a power-house in the early 1970s. At Easter 1973 it held a conference, 'What Kind of Scotland', in George Square Theatre, Edinburgh. To this John McGrath's 7:84 troupe came with a hastily written play which was to pack as much punch as the *Three Estates* had 433 years earlier, particularly when it played around the Highlands. McGrath's position was uncompromisingly leftist, but in the face of big oil and wobbly Whitehall, the lessons drawn from it were as much nationalist as socialist.

resolutely refused to let the Nationalists lay claim to his play and indeed exco-riated the SNP, a good many of those who saw it concluded that the only chance of implementing its implicit message lay with independence.

And not just in the Highlands. The people of Central Scotland were strug-gling with change too. The blood was slowly draining out of Scotland's old economic muscle. Between 1970 and 1974 the number of coal mines fell by a third, and steel production declined by a fifth. The new electronics industry, much of which was American-owned, did not want trade-unionised labour and tended to employ more women than men. Local government reform, proposed by another Royal Commission chaired by Lord Wheatley, meant dozens of familiar little councils being swept away and replaced by more anonymous larger district and regional councils. It may have been efficient but many towns thought they were being wiped off the map. Fife councillors evoked centuries of history to stop the 'kingdom' being divided and ruled from Dundee and Edinburgh.

III

Into all this, the Kilbrandon Commission report did what it wasn't supposed to do, and landed with a mighty splash. Despite three years of labour, its members failed to come up with a unanimous verdict, an indirect compliment to Scottish politicians who were equally divided. The members were agreed that there should be directly elected assemblies, elected by proportional repre-sentation. The majority thought that the Scottish and Welsh assemblies should have legislative powers (as the Scottish parliament now has) and a minority that they should only be responsible for implementing laws passed at Westminster (as now is the Welsh Assembly). A dissenting report called for the same degree of devolution to five English regions, a federalist solution.

The Nationalists and Liberals enthused about the majority position. The Scottish Tories, who had dumped their support for an assembly earlier in the year, were sceptical. The Scottish Labour Party, having just published a pamphlet scornful of devolution and suggesting tinkering with Scottish committees at Westminster, was hostile. Kilbrandon might have sunk, but its ripples were suddenly swamped by another boulder landing in the pool – Govan.

Labour had at least picked a local man for the parliamentary by-election, a veteran Trotskyist barber, Harry Selby, but this was only because many of the members of the small constituency party were his relatives. The SNP picked Margo MacDonald, a big, brassy, blonde who was working-class and proud of it. She told it as she saw it and the voters in Govan, who were only too well aware of the miserable state their housing had sunk to under Labour's municipal control, flocked to her. Her victory did not, however, have the impact that

A VOTER'S GUIDE
to the

SCOTTISH

ASSEMBLY

and

WHY YOU SHOULD
SUPPORT IT

(25p)

Figure 6.6
'The hair, my dear, and those views!'
Photograph provided by *The Scotsman.*
Assorted young Labour candidates present
themselves, headed by the editor of *The
Red Paper on Scotland* pictured with fellow
student radicals in 1975. A cooperative
effort by Labour left-wingers, Communists
and SNPers, the paper looked and
sometimes read like a telephone directory.
Its scarlet politics irrupted thereafter more
on the Scottish left, although Gordon
Brown, then Rector of Edinburgh University
(at 23!), has become a byword for
front-bench sobriety.

Winnie Ewing's did, for the country was soon gripped by the crisis and the three-day working week caused by Edward Heath's battles with striking miners and power workers.

In the general election of February 1974, Harold Wilson was returned to Downing Street, but without a majority, making another election a certainty. But the landscape of Scottish politics had changed dramatically. While MacDonald lost her seat, the SNP had won six, two from Labour (including Dundee East) and four from the Tories. Wilson, studying the results and the polls which indicated that about a dozen Labour seats were vulnerable to the SNP, concluded devolution was the answer and promised a white paper. He had, however, a little local difficulty – the Scottish party leadership.

Figure 6.7 Lord Kilbrandon.
Photograph provided by *The Herald*.
Kilbrandon had pioneered the reform of the juvenile courts in the 1960s. Harold Wilson made him deputy to the conservative economist Lord Crowther on the Royal Commission on the Constitution, 1969, and he succeeded Crowther when the latter died. Wilson hoped the Commission would put the issue to sleep. Instead, Kilbrandon woke it up. Here he is campaigning for a 'yes' vote in the 1979 referendum with the Reverend David Steel, father of the Liberal leader, Farquhar Mackintosh, Rector of the Royal High School, Ludovic Kennedy and a subsequent apostate, Sir Donald MacKay.

But cracks had appeared in this monolith of unionism. For months before the election, four Labour MPs – Jim Sillars, Harry Ewing, Alex Eadie and John Robertson – had been arguing the case for devolution with other MPs and winning converts. Even Willie Ross was softening the language of opposition.

Figure 6.8
Margo MacDonald campaigning in Govan in 1973. Photograph provided by *The Herald*. The Govan by-election, caused by the death of the veteran and somewhat nationalist-inclined Labour MP John Rankin, was fought for Labour by Harry Selby, a Trotskyist barber (a less unusual combination than it might appear). The SNP fielded Margo MacDonald, as striking a performer as Winnie Ewing, and like her making the eventual transformation from 'blonde bombshell' to *grande dame*. Willie Ross had just christened the Kilbrandon Report the 'Kill-devolution' report, a Labour revulsion which lasted only a week. MacDonald won.

Figure 6.9 The Bay City Rollers: fans go crazy.
Photograph provided by *The Herald*.
There had been nothing like it since the 'teenies met Davy Crockett in the mid-1950s. In *Little Red Hen* John McGrath guyed the SNP as the Rollers of Scottish politics with their tartan-clad fans. What did it mean? Those wee girls will all now be in their late thirties . . .

A month after the election, the Scottish Labour executive reversed its stance against 'any new-fangled Assembly' adopted under ludicrous circumstances the previous summer. (Only eleven of twenty-eight members had turned up to that meeting, the stay-aways preferring to watch the televised Scotland v Yugoslavia football match, and the result was 6–5 against devolution. The five included Donald Dewar and George Robertson, then regarded as dangerous radicals.) Now the executive said an Assembly 'perhaps' and 'might' be a good idea.

Wilson wanted 'yes' and instructed the Scottish executive to recall the Scottish conference, which met in August 1974 in the Glasgow Cooperative Hall in Dalintober Street. This name was to be evoked for years afterwards as a sort of Tiananmen Square-style crushing of innocent constituency democracy beneath the tank tracks of union block votes. The unions were certainly drilled to vote for an Assembly by Alex Kitson, a Transport and General Workers Union fixer and an old home ruler. As Alex Donnett, of the General and Municipal Workers Union, said, if devolution was the price for getting a majority Labour government, so be it. But as the unions had only half the delegates present and the motion was carried overwhelmingly, the constituency and other delegates must have played along.

The irony was that the Scottish Labour Party, which in the 1980s and 1990s regarded itself as the guardian of the devolution flame against any backsliding

Figure 6.10 The face of the future? The SNP parliamentary group.
Photograph provided by Gordon Wright Photo Library.
In 1974, after two indecisive elections and a rise in their vote to 30 per cent and eleven MPs, are the SNP only 6 per cent away from a breakthrough?

Figure 6.11 Stephen Maxwell wins in Wester Hailes, 1976.
Photograph provided by Gordon Wright Photo Library.
Stephen Maxwell, from Cambridge and Chatham House, head of publicity for the SNP, is chaired by SNP
supporters after winning a Wester Hailes regional council seat from Labour in 1976, a point at which it looked
as if Labour's control of Scotland was collapsing day by day.

by the UK leadership, was shotgunned into devolution *by* that leadership.
Wilson went back to the country in October, and this time secured a majority
of just three seats. In Scotland, Labour gained one seat from the Tories, Berwick
and East Lothian, to hold forty-one, while the Tories slumped to just sixteen.

IV

But the big Scottish story was the seemingly relentless onward march of
Nationalism. The SNP gained four seats, all from the Tories, to have a parliamentary group of eleven, rivalling the Liberal group of thirteen drawn from all
over Britain. Even more impressive was the record of votes won. From an 11 per
cent share of the vote in 1970, the SNP moved to 22 per cent in February 1974

and 30 per cent in October. Its growth had been exponential and unprecedented in British politics. Moreover, although Wilson's finessing of the devolution issue had held Labour's position in Scotland, the SNP was now in second place in thirty-four Labour-held seats, menacingly so in eleven of them.

The weakness of Labour's position was that it had always based its appeal to Scottish voters on being able to use the strength of the British state for Scotland's benefit. Now, however, it was being outbid and outflanked by the SNP because of the oil card. Quite noticeably, the SNP now had a heartland in North-east Scotland – Moray and Nairn, Banffshire, East Aberdeenshire, Angus East, Perth and East Perthshire, and Dundee East – where the voters could reasonably be thought to have the oil issue at the forefront of their minds.

Oil interests were, for a time, genuinely concerned that a Scottish breakaway was possible, but soon switched their attention to the predatory activities of the British Labour government and the alarming Tony Benn (actually half-Scots himself), whom Wilson had made industry minister and then, in 1975, energy minister. The SNP initially benefited from the upheaval of local government regionalisation, carried through in 1974, but could not make a permanent impact.

For a while, the political spotlight swung towards Europe and the referendum on Wilson's renegotiated terms of British membership of the European Economic Community (EEC). The left – socialist and nationalist – got the European issue almost totally wrong. The British or Scottish states were seen as bulwarks against European 'interference'; the Labour left thought favourably of a sort of 'war socialism'; the SNP wanted to follow parallels with Norway (which used its oil and fishing interests to gain some access to the European common market but paid none of the costs of EEC membership) – but they failed to get their way in the 1975 referendum. Scotland turned out only slightly less European than the South. The ultimately corrosive effect on British Conservatism that Europe was to have was almost completely unanticipated.

Labour's capitulation to devolution in the 1970s could be seen as a wimpish surrender to *force majeure*. It was the low-cost solution to a horribly expensive problem. But it coincided with a Europe-wide perplexity; regionalism moved out to challenge the centralised nation-state, from the Basque terrorists who blew Franco's Prime Minister Admiral Carrero Blanco to bits in 1973 to the Bretons and the benign modernisation of the Communist city-states of central Italy. The EEC's development posed its own conundrum here. As power seeped upwards to Brussels from once-sovereign nation-states, should the regions seek their own relationship with Europe, and if so, what kind of relationship? For once, Scotland seemed to have moved abreast of a general European development, something celebrated in the philosophical polemic of Tom Nairn as well as in the clotted sociology of the American Michael Hechter's *Internal Colonialism: the Celtic Fringe in British National Development* (1975). In the 1960s nationalists had been uncouth interrupters; now they were trendy, and got to strut their stuff at conferences and on the box. For a time . . .

V

If it was not obvious in opposition, it became glaringly apparent in government that Harold Wilson had major difficulties in convincing his parliamentary party of the merits of devolution. There was pragmatic opposition from North-east of England MPs who were worried that Scotland would get a huge advantage in dealing with the problems of declining heavy industry which the

Figure 6.12 Jim Sillars campaigns for a 'yes' vote in 1979.
Photograph provided by *The Scotsman*.
Jim Sillars was all that remained by 1979 of the Scottish Labour Party. Here he tries to keep 'Yes for Scotland' afloat in the referendum campaign of 1979, with Margo MacDonald, whom he would marry, the Reverend Duncan Shaw, Professor Nigel Grant and Donald Gorrie.

North-east equally faced. And there was principled opposition from the left, who saw devolution as a brand of nationalism which cut through the solidarity of the working classes and undermined the ability of the state to deliver benefits to the working classes. The latter's chief cheerleader was Neil Kinnock, whose disloyalty in honing his oratorical and parliamentary skills from the back benches against devolution, oddly enough, gave him a reputation that was the foundation for becoming the Labour leader in 1983. His followers were undeterred by the fact that soon after Margaret Thatcher took the Tory leadership from Heath, her party abandoned its feeble devolution policy and resolved to oppose Labour's Assembly plans root and branch.

The SNP MPs were at this stage relegated to support player status, committed to supporting devolution as the first step towards independence. The problems the government faced were all internal. Cabinet dissension delayed the promised white paper until November 1975. It faced such a torrent of criticism – over a proposed rates surcharge power and powers given to the Scottish Secretary to veto Assembly legislation – that the government had to issue a revised version the following August.

That was too late to prevent two Labour MPs – Jim Sillars and John Robertson – from breaking away to set up the Scottish Labour Party. The ostensible reason was that the proposed Assembly lacked the 'economic teeth' promised in the election manifesto, but there were other reasons – the powerlessness of the Scottish party over Scottish policy and the perversion of democracy represented by trade union block votes. The 'magic party' won plenty of publicity, not least because some of Scotland's leading political journalists were involved in it, but not a lot else. It succeeded only in sucking in Trotskyite far left groups such as the International Marxist Group, then choked on them as Sillars moved to expel entryists at the party's shambolic conference at Stirling in 1976. By late 1977, the party was dead. Both Sillars and Robertson lost their seats at the 1979 election.

VI

At Westminster, the revised white paper removed the Scottish Secretary's veto power, but no tax-raising power was offered. The Assembly's economic powers were clarified to include power over the new Scottish Development Agency, set up in 1975. But the resulting Scotland and Wales Bill met obdurate opposition, mainly from English MPs who seemed surprised at the sweeping constitutional changes it envisaged. When the government sought to push the bill through on a strict timetable, twenty-two Labour MPs (only two were Scottish and two were Welsh) rebelled against the guillotine. The government retreated to think again.

Figure 6.13
Scotland says No!
Photograph
provided by *The
Scotsman.*
Someone has
been at this copy
of a 'Scotland
says No!'
poster . . . The
anti-devolution
cause united
forces – which
would otherwise
have been at
each other's
throats – and
came within an
ace of winning
a majority on
1 March 1979,
though a
technical
knockout
sufficed.

By this time, Wilson had resigned and James Callaghan had become Prime Minister. Defections and by-elections had whittled Labour's majority away, and Callaghan negotiated a pact with the Liberals to buy himself more time in office. The Liberals exacted separate bills for Scottish and Welsh devolution. They were duly introduced and ground their way through the Commons, occupying hours and hours of time, week after week. It was scant consolation to the Callaghan government, as it was harassed and harried by rebellious back-benchers, that the Tories were also divided over devolution. Malcolm

Rifkind and Alick Buchanan-Smith had resigned from Margaret Thatcher's shadow team, and with a small number of back-benchers, including Ian Lang, pursued their own pro-devolution line. But grind on it did, for the May 1977 local elections saw the SNP make big gains, winning 131 seats from Labour, depriving it of control even of Glasgow. The Labour Party knew what fate awaited them if they abandoned the Assembly. Despite this pressing political imperative, Tam Dalyell, MP for West Lothian, persisted and became forever identified with the most (in)famous conundrum of the devolution debate. Why, he wanted to know, was it right that he and the other seventy-one Scottish MPs could, post-Assembly, debate and vote on education matters in Blackburn, Lancashire, but not on the same matters in Blackburn, West Lothian? Nothing said by John Smith, appointed as a junior minister in the Cabinet Office to steer the bill through, could reassure him. Dalyell asked the question so often, and always in the most contorted fashion, that an exasperated Michael Foot suggested that if he just called it the West Lothian question, a great deal of time would be saved. So it became known, but answer came there none.

Eventually, the government was forced to concede that there should be a referendum before the Assembly could be enacted. And into this concession to democracy was built a profoundly undemocratic tripwire. George Cunningham, an anti-devolution Scot and Labour MP for Islington South, successfully moved that at least 40 per cent of the whole electorate had to vote 'yes', otherwise the Act would have to be repealed. In every other British election or plebiscite, a simple majority has sufficed, but in this case a rule which effectively meant that those who did not bother to vote would be counted as 'no' votes was invoked. With a sinking heart, pro-devolutionists prepared for the referendum on 1 March 1979.

Still, it might have been all right on the night if the government had not been plunging deep into economic disaster. The problem was that the international spasm of stagflation triggered initially by the Arab use of the oil weapon hit Britain peculiarly hard, as the Labour government had to import vast amounts of material for the exploitation of the North Sea fields at a point where inflation and public spending seemed close to getting out of control. The resulting exertion of the International Monetary Fund's will over the British government

Figure 6.14 Devolution: lever for change. (opposite)
Poster provided by Christopher Harvie.
A poster from the 1979 referendum campaign which some bright spark based on Russian revolutionary propaganda. This Lissitzky-like work was designed to urge the Scots masses to vote for devolution on 1 March 1979. But just as the impact of the Russian avant-garde was overestimated, so too was the drawing power of the Callaghan–Millan package. The reality was that the leaflets produced by the 'yes' side were small and crabbit, and after the fruitless vote hundreds of bundles were found dumped in union and party offices because there was no one to deliver them.

in 1976 apparently exposed the powerlessness of the British state against the international market. Reactions to the measures then imposed by Denis Healey, Chancellor, split Labour from top to bottom.

Curiously, and perhaps because the Scotland Act was nearing the statute book, Labour in Scotland recovered its nerve in 1978 and enjoyed a run of success against the SNP which, in any case, was suffering from the stresses and strains of trying to be both a pro-devolution parliamentary party at Westminster and a populist pro-independence campaigning party in Scotland. While the MPs were swallowing the unacceptable, such as the 40 per cent rule, in order to keep the devolution show on the road, activists in Scotland were arguing that the party should abandon the whole caboodle and campaign for a 'no' vote. Labour also revived the 'tartan Tories' epithet and made it stick in west Central Scotland thanks to the failure of Nationalist MPs to vote for a shipbuilding nationalisation bill.

Figure 6.15 Scottish fans dig up the Wembley turf, summer 1977.
Photograph provided by *The Herald*.
This was the real climax of the old booze-powered Tartan Army, before they sobered up and became the dolls of the European game. Presiding over this mayhem can be seen the grand old hooligan himself, Rod Stewart. Having beaten England, the fans thought the World Cup lay at their feet.

Figure 6.16 Ally's Tartan Army meets its Bannockburn then its Flodden.
Photograph provided by *The Herald*.
Perhaps it wasn't a good idea to pose with an equally doomed car, the Hillman Avenger, which turned out to be the last wheeled thing produced at Linwood. 'We wis magic' in 1977 at Wembley. 'We wis rubbish' – definitely – in Argentina. Would a win (or at least not being defeated by Peru) have carried the 'yes' vote?

Against this background, Labour's Donald Dewar defeated the SNP in a parliamentary by-election in Glasgow Garscadden; not even Margo MacDonald could stop George Robertson winning another by-election in Hamilton; and John Home Robertson easily saw off the SNP in a third contest at Berwickshire and East Lothian. Picking able and articulate candidates undoubtedly helped, as did the divisions in the SNP. But the referendum campaign was a different matter. All sorts of reasons have been advanced to explain why the outcome was a long way short of being a big endorsement of the Scottish Assembly. Did the Scottish football team's abysmal performance in the 1978 World Cup in Argentina have anything to do with it? Your authors are divided on this one, but in general the 'no' campaigners appeared to have more weight on their side; the dedicated application of Gordon Brown and his coterie of zealous student activists was no match for the fanatical unionism of Tam Dalyell, related by marriage to that stalwart of Catholic Unionism Lord Wheatley, as well as descended from the scourge of the Covenanters, Black Tam of the Binns.

The fact that the parties were divided did not help. (Labour's Robin Cook, and Brian Wilson were prominent 'no' campaigners; the Tories' Malcolm Rifkind and Alick Buchanan-Smith were equally prominent 'yes' campaigners while Lord Home, the Tory ex-Prime Minister, further confused things by urging a 'no' vote so that the Tories could bring in a better devolution bill.) And the fact that most employers and some big institutions such as the universities were hostile to devolution must have counted against the 'yes' campaigners, as did the fact that independence, hoped by the SNP and feared by the Assembly's opponents to be the destination at the foot of devolution's slippery slope, was unpopular with the electorate.

VII

But the overriding factor was the collapse of public confidence in the Labour government brought about by the 'winter of discontent'. Anger at the government's pay restraint policy, brought in to try and bring down inflation which was running at above 10 per cent for the first time since 1972, boiled over. Car workers went on strike in October 1978, print workers downed tools in December, lorry drivers, hospital and other public sector workers struck in January 1979, and even civil servants walked out in February. The impression given by uncollected rubbish piling up on skating rink-like streets, patients going without treatment and the dead going unburied, was that chaos had descended and the government had lost control. Why then, should the voters have any confidence that this Assembly would be good for them when not even all the government's own MPs wanted it?

And on polling day, it snowed. In the event, 64 per cent of the electorate did make it to the ballot box, and of them, 51.6 per cent voted 'yes'. It was a majority, but it fell far short of the 40 per cent target. Generally speaking, a third of Scots voted 'yes', a third voted 'no' and a third could not be bothered. Frantically the government wheeled and dealed, trying to avoid putting the order repealing the devolution legislation to a vote in the Commons. An exasperated SNP, trying to issue an ultimatum to the government, put down a censure motion which Margaret Thatcher eagerly latched on to. On 28 March, the government lost by 311 votes to 310. Harold Wilson later wrote laconically: 'If, for a time, it was rotten garbage that threatened the Labour government, it was devolution that forced it to the country . . . and the country gave its answer on May 3rd.'

The Scottish media, then principally *The Scotsman*, *The Glasgow Herald* and the *Daily Record*, was aghast. They had invested heavily in devolution and had discovered that the public did not share their obsession. There was much lamentation that the Scots had suffered a failure of nerve. A longer-term view suggests a different perspective. The bill about which the Scots were so lukewarm was a bad bill. The Assembly was to be handed down its powers in a way which would have made constant conflict with Westminster inevitable. The Scotland Act wrote down definitions of everything that the Assembly could do; anything else was outside its power. But the nature of government changes constantly, and it changed dramatically in the 1980s. That would have necessitated constant rewriting of the Assembly's powers and each such rewrite would have provoked accusations of Westminster encroachment in much the same way that the

REGION / ISLANDS AREA	YES VOTES	NO VOTES
WESTERN ISLES	6,218	4,933
DUMFRIES & GALLOWAY	27,162	40,239
SHETLAND ISLANDS	2,020	5,466
CENTRAL	71,296	59,105
FIFE	86,252	74,436
ORKNEY ISLANDS	2,104	5,439
BORDERS	20,746	30,780
TAYSIDE	91,482	93,325
GRAMPIAN	94,944	101,485
LOTHIAN	187,221	186,421
STRATHCLYDE	596,519	508,599
HIGHLAND	44,973	43,274
TOTAL	1,230,937	1,153,502

Figure 6.17 The referendum result, 1979.
Photograph provided by *The Scotsman*.
Reading out the results of the 1 March referendum. The 'left' polled depressingly low. Lothian was almost equally divided, with Robin Cook trying to put the 'no' vote ahead and Malcolm Rifkind trying to prevent him. Fancy that!

Figure 6.18 'A Senate in Waiting?'
Photograph provided by the SNP.
Royal High School's hall after the boys had gone and before the Assemblymen (didn't) arrive. Thomas Hamilton's 1829 building was handsome and – given later developments – cheap. But its narrow galleries wouldn't have given the public much of a look-in.

European Union is constantly accused of encroaching on British sovereignty, only of a more intense and acrimonious nature, with the SNP cast in the role that the Tories have taken on with regard to Europe.

Neither did the Assembly have any power to raise its own taxes. This is an essential responsibility, for without it, politicians simply pass the blame for their own failings to those who control the purse strings. And the Assembly was to be elected by the first-past-the-post method, which would have ensured Central Scotland Labour Party domination and left the Highlands and Borders feeling marginalised.

Under these circumstances – division within Scotland, division and buck-passing between Edinburgh and London – it is entirely reasonable to imagine the entire exercise collapsing in rancorous disillusion. It was misconceived as an expedient way of dealing with a political threat rather than as a search for a better system of government. It was misconstructed; despite the efforts of Scottish ministers such as John Smith at the Cabinet Office and Harry Ewing at the Scottish Office, the bill was always being retailored to pacify English MPs' opinion. It could easily have ended with a grateful Scottish electorate thanking Margaret Thatcher for taking this London-imposed contraption away and comforting themselves with the thought that they had not really wanted it in the first place.

CHAPTER SEVEN

Thatcher's Other Country

I believe that the British State is to be categorised as an *ancien régime*. It is closer in spirit to the monarchy overthrown in 1789 than to the republican constitutions which followed in France and elsewhere in Europe. It is true that French Jacobin republicanism introduced – or perhaps reinforced – a rigid centralisation of power which has some parallels in the extreme overcentralisation of modern Britain. But it also established the doctrine of popular sovereignty, based on the notion of the rights of man, expressed in a constitution of supreme authority to which the citizen could – in theory – appeal over the heads even of the National Assembly. I am arguing here for a British version of republicanism, and it is my view that while Jacobin centralism is exceptional among republican projects, the principle of popular sovereignty and a written constitution is an almost universal element of definition.

Neal Ascherson, 1986

Yince there was a king, wha sat,
Scrievin' this edict in his palace-haa:
Vassals, I tell ye flat,
That I am I, and ye are bugger-aa!

Ugo Belli, translated by Robert Garioch,
1960, in Garioch, *Collected Poems*, 1981

I

Things after 1979 were very different. Margaret Thatcher has been credited as the 'onlie begetter' of Scottish home rule, *the* person who made the Scots think that the differences from the South, not the similarities, determined their nation. But could there not have been a market for a Scottish Thatcherism? The window of opportunity for it was wide open; the SNP had experienced a Culloden-type defeat (reduced to two seats) and would spend five years at war with itself; the Labour Party was similarly exhausted, fed up with devolution and spiralling into factional conflict. Moreover, Thatcherism had an intellectual bridgehead in Scotland at St Andrews University. Under the mentorship of Ralph, later Lord Harris, an economics lecturer at the university in the 1950s

Figure 7.1 George Younger and Scottish Conservative candidates in 1979.
Photograph provided by *The Herald*.
During a break in their campaign meeting they pose for a memorable photograph outside their HQ on the eve of battle. Within twenty years they were virtually an extinct species.

who maintained his connections after moving to London, and the historian Professor Norman Gash, a group of Tory students took to the lucid simplicities of Friedrich von Hayek and Milton Friedman.

These St Andrews individualists had a practical and even populist line remote from Hayek's rather dotty utopianism; they persuaded Heath to legalise pirate radio – rusty ships in the North Sea transmitting what people wanted to hear, not what the BBC thought they ought to hear. Two of them, Madsen Pirie and Eamon Butler, went on to found the Adam Smith Institute, claiming Scottish roots for this thinking. They liked to think of themselves as Thatcher's court philosophers (though she was far from being an intellectual, and Pirie

Figure 7.2
'Man, greatest of all the beasts of the earth for pride'. Copyright: Alasdair Gray. Provided by the Trustees of the National Library of Scotland.
Alasdair Gray's vision of industrial Scotland from *Lanark*, 1982. Besides encapsulating the busy but problematic heart of Central Scotland, Gray's panorama shows the distance between Scots civic communitarianism and the menacing figure of Thomas Hobbes' *Leviathan*, symbol of absolute sovereignty, whether of monarch or of parliament.

said they did better with John Major). A third, Michael Forsyth, was to spend much of his political career at the Scottish Office.

Despite a rhetoric of resistance to Thatcher, her determination and many of her ploys often went down well. George Foulkes MP found that the much-loved Shirley Williams nodded and smiled sweetly and did nothing, while Thatcher glared and argued and acted. The Scots accepted, grudgingly, transfers from the failing and feckless to the 'enterprising', and the winding-down of the remaining heavy industries. Labour realised that council house sales (to which Thatcher was initially opposed) were popular, a policy which revolutionised housing tenure, moving owner occupation from under one-third to nearly two-thirds. The notion that financial services and information technology would dominate the country's economy, scarcely credible in 1979, was commonplace in 1989. Aggregate living standards rose faster in Scotland than anywhere else in Britain apart from the South-east; by 1997 Scotland almost rivalled the London area. But the voters were unconvinced. The fact that, as leader of the opposition, Thatcher had been popular in Scotland, being greeted by cheering crowds in Glasgow, was tactfully disremembered.

Thatcher was for much of the time pragmatic and *étatiste*. 'All power is marvellous. Absolute power is absolutely marvellous,' Julian Critchley imagined her saying. Monetarism's horrors could be dumped on Sir Geoffrey Howe and she was well minded by the amiable Whitelaw – 'No prime minister should be without a Willie,' as she remarked in an unforgettable tribute. What then went wrong for the Conservatives? At one level they fell foul of a rather old-fashioned Gladstonian moralistic rejection of the harder manifestations of individualism and such jingo episodes as the Falklands War. Thanks to the increasingly internationalised as well as privatised nature of Conservatism, the gains of the winners were banked discreetly and abroad, realised in exclusive homes and foreign holidays. This helped the financiers and bankers of Charlotte Square in Edinburgh, who used the wealth earned from North Sea oil corporate work to build Scottish finance into a European force and to create tens of thousands of jobs. But there were no wealthy benefactors of the common weal like the hospital and school founders of Victorian capitalism, and a strong whiff of what David Marquand called 'the unprincipled society'. Although Thatcher lurched into ethics from time to time, she blotted her copybook at one strategically important moment – just before her address to the Fathers and Brethren of the Kirk in 1988 – by denying that society existed at all. The state-sector middle class and a dramatically divided working class – both rather more important than they were in the south – were particularly hard-hit by Howe's budgets, designed to curb welfare spending, prune the state sector and encourage private enterprise. But Tory canvassers in the 1987 election were alarmed to discover how often on middle-class doorsteps rants about 'that

Figure 7.3 Mrs Thatcher's 'Sermon on the Mound' in May 1988. Photograph provided by *The Herald*. She never got the joke, any more than (on the same visit) she understood why Celtic fans waved Irish tricolours. But her simplistic *laissez-faire* rhetoric provoked a confrontation with the 'Fathers and Brethren', which in some ways accounted for the Kirk's subsequent radicalism on the constitution.

bloody woman' (heard so often that Tories shortened it to TBW) concentrated on 'her English voice'. In a way this was a delayed outcome of the nationalist excitements of the 1970s; the remarkable revival of an especially urban and anti-establishment art and literature made her painful elocution look terribly old hat.

In 1979 Glasgow Cathcart rejected Thatcher's champion in Scotland, Teddy Taylor, whose populist forthrightness might well have made a difference. Instead, she sought 'a safe pair of hands' at the Scottish Office in George Younger (kin to the brewing dynasty, heir to a viscount but also nephew of a Labour MP). Younger, with a near-permanent Oor Wullie grin, was approachable and a master of manœuvre. Many a delegation would enter his office, grim-faced and determined to be unyielding, and come away charmed, convinced that they had successfully made their case. Only later would they realise that they had secured nothing.

Younger served a long six-year stint, seeing the Tories through the 1983 election in which their vote slipped only marginally from 32 per cent to 28 per cent, losing one seat, Glasgow Hillhead – and not to Labour or the SNP, but to the new Social Democrat Party. Roy Jenkins, the former Labour minister and European Commission president, won it at a by-election and held on to it. His voters, a lot of them lecturers and students at the university, took to the SDP like Home Counties suburbanites, and with rather uneasy Liberals forged an Alliance to contest the 1983 and 1987 elections. It also looked for a time as if they might win over the traditionally right-wing Catholic Labour vote.

Younger punched his weight among businessmen and was (like that other patrician Whitelaw) shrewder than he looked. He could turn on a Macmillanite style to entrance aggressive reporters or ingratiate party members. Industrial traumas were painful necessities, but he would help Scotland to thole them. Where Thatcher dismantled the English metropolitan councils and ultimately the Greater London Council, Younger rescued Strathclyde Regional Council, the next biggest local authority in Europe. He gave its pragmatic Lanarkshire Labourites money and they kept quiet. Even that craggiest of trade unionists, Mick McGahey, the Communist Scottish miners' leader, recalled him with affection, even after the bitter miners' strike. After McGahey's less than successful attempt to win a seat on Ayr Council, Younger said to him: 'I saw your result, Mick. Was that your age or your vote?'

II

Younger might have been Gilmour or Maclay. Had Scotland therefore retreated from the excitements of nationalism? But a continuing 'Scottish identity' meant that public opinion was filtered through institutions which allowed for a greater flexibility of responses by the political élite, left and right. The STUC complained about centralised Thatcherite control but, while it lost its quango seats, it never lost its position in Scottish society as the TUC did south of the border. Nor were local authorities, apart from one or two spats over money, projected as run by loony crackpots, as they were in England. The education

Figure 7.4 Mick McGahey. Portrait by Maggie Hambling. Provided by the Scottish National Portrait Gallery. The miners go back to work after a bitter strike nearly a year long which had been mismanaged by the militant Arthur Scargill. Warm and dignified, the Scots Communist leader Mick McGahey, by contrast, became a sort of folk hero. Chairman of the Scottish Miners, McGahey was in libertarian terms no political oil painting. Yet in the strike of 1984–5, his diplomatic moderation contrasted with the unyielding attitude of Scargill, and subsequently he made his dying union into a national symbol of the damage inflicted by Thatcherite rationalisation.

and health élites, apart from Forsyth's brief irruption into their domain, continued to run things in a decent, even complacent fashion, as did the lawyers. There was still a kind of underground autonomy about Scottish affairs which Thatcherism never reached. The English march-in-step of triumphant populist Toryism and the media – itself the work of such mischievous North Britons as Rupert Murdoch and his lieutenants, Kelvin MacKenzie of *The Sun* and Andrew

Neil of *The Sunday Times* – was lacking. The *Daily Record* took after *The Herald* and *The Scotsman*, in contrast to England where even the broadsheets were fascinated by the lively brutality of the tabloids.

This difference was noticed, and often cursed (to no effect), by Scottish Tories, but other differences were more subtle and less detectable. In 1983 the Social Democrat impact hit the right and the SNP, not the left. Labour could recover, not least because it loosened its ties with its rather embarrassing allies in the trade unions, who had largely been excluded from the new manufacturing industries. European regionalism was also getting into its stride in the mid-1980s, and the large-scale Scottish local authorities made their presence felt. As London retreated from Scottish infrastructural and industrial policy, Brussels more than symbolically moved in. Strathclyde Regional Council, pragmatically ignoring Labour's ideological doubts about Europe, pioneered the art of extracting soothingly large sums of money from the Eurocrats.

Early Thatcherism was dominated by the issue of the 'smokestack' industries, savagely hit by her experiments in monetarism. This coincided with the Iranian revolution and the first Gulf War, which pushed the oil price up to almost $40 a barrel. The result was a petro-pound so high as to cut British manufacturing industry by almost a fifth. This carried away many of the brave attempts to broaden the Scottish industrial base, such as the Corpach pulp mill and the Invergordon aluminium smelter, as well as the rather forlorn attempt to establish a motor vehicle industry at Linwood and Bathgate, always a dubious proposition because of their distance from Midlands-based component suppliers.

As a result the future of such capital goods industries as coal and steel was put on the line. After a preliminary steel strike in 1981, when workers' solidarity wasn't much in evidence, the confrontation came in the attrition warfare of the miners' strike in 1984–5. In its aftermath Scottish miners' numbers tumbled from 10 000 to a few hundred, with most coal being clawed out of the ground in opencast sites. State sector firms were rationalised and sold off. This realised vast sums for the Treasury and shifted the economic balance remorselessly towards the private sector, where trade union militancy suffered a slow death by piecemeal removal of its weaponry and rising unemployment.

Where once the builders of the new Jerusalem had been the planners, now they were the entrepreneurs. Scottish businessmen vigorously applauded this shift in industrial politics in favour of management and shareholders. Privatisation of the utilities, especially the sell-off of British Gas and its clever 'Tell Sid' marketing campaign, persuaded so many to join the great share rush that there was talk of a new shareholder democracy. Most Sids, in fact, flogged their shares as soon as they rose in value, but this and the relaxation of takeover regulations had a predictable knock-on effect. The fluidity in the stock market encouraged share-dealing entrepreneurs to look around for companies that could be bought up cheaply and then rationalised, usually by cutting jobs and selling off ill-fitting subsidiary activities.

What was not predictable were the side-effects in Scotland, where business-men suddenly stopped applauding. An early taste of this was the battle for the Royal Bank of Scotland in 1981. First, Standard Chartered Bank, which was a British bank with most of its business in the Middle East and South Africa, and then the Hong Kong and Shanghai Bank, an East Asian giant, bid for the Royal. The prospect that control of the Royal might disappear to London or even further afield alarmed other Scottish financial institutions, as it did George Younger and his industry minister Alex Fletcher. Fletcher's reasoning was that if an enterprise economy was to take root, it would need finance which was more likely to come from a bank controlled in Edinburgh than one run from Hong Kong. Fletcher persuaded John Biffen, Trade and Industry Secretary, to refer the bids to the Monopolies and Mergers Commission, which duly recommended that the bids be rejected on the grounds that the public interest might be damaged. In fact, this meant the 'Scottish public interest' and effectively put up a large hands-off notice around Scottish financial companies.

And there was quite a lot of this intervention around. When the government decided to sell its holding in Ferranti, an electronics firm which employed about 7000 Scots, the likelihood was that it would be bought up by GEC or Racal, which would pursue job cuts and rationalisation. The STUC duly cranked up a campaign against the sell-off, and Fletcher used this to persuade the government that a straight sale was politically unacceptable. The shares were eventually sold with so many strings attached as to make a bid impossible. Similarly, when Weir Engineering was threatened with bankruptcy following the closure of Linwood, the Scottish Office helped magic its bank debts into preference shares which could be sold, giving the company vital breathing-space. There was logic behind this cavalier disregard for market rigour – both firms were at the high-technology end of electrical engineering, the type of industry which the Tories were insisting represented Scotland's future.

Indeed, had existing industrial Scotland a future? The giant American-owned Singer factory at Clydebank, which once employed 23 000 and still had 4500 employees in 1979, closed. More foreign-owned factories shut their doors in rapid succession: Monsanto chemicals in Ayrshire, Pye TMC electronics in Livingston, VF Corporation in Greenock, Massey Ferguson at Kilmarnock. The term 'branch economy syndrome' entered political debate, meaning that when the going got rough in the world economy, as in the early 1980s, factories distant from company bases in faraway places like Scotland were the first to be lopped off. The massive effort put into luring new foreign investment did yield returns, but the new jobs arriving were disturbingly fewer than the old jobs disappearing.

Younger and Fletcher were acutely aware of the problem and, from day one, they constantly banged out the message that Scots had to look to the new sunrise industries of electronics and finance for new jobs. There was much political skirmishing around inward investment. Fletcher and most of the Tories felt that the Scottish Development Agency's (SDA's) overseas promotion work was all bagpipes and haggis and the job could be better done by the Foreign Office embassy network. Robin Duthie, installed as a more 'friendly' chairman of the SDA, turned out to be not at all compliant. People in London knew nothing of how serious Scotland's economic plight was, he said, and insisted that Scotland had to be marketed as a single entity. He won when Fletcher decided to merge the SDA and Scottish Office teams into a single-door Locate in Scotland agency. Younger had learned from Willie Ross how to confront Whitehall. *The Daily Telegraph* in 1984 quoted a Cabinet colleague as saying that Younger would depict Scotland 'as an industrial graveyard down to its last national assets and then intimidate us with the bogey of separatism'.

Scottish businessmen were far more worried about predatory bogeymen, and there were plenty of them about. Belhaven Brewery was taken over by Eric Morley, the 'Miss World' contest promoter; Lindustries, a textile manufacturer, was acquired by Hanson Trust; House of Fraser, with its chain of department stores, lost a long battle against Lonrho's predations; Anderson Strathclyde, a mining equipment maker, rapidly succumbed to Charter Consolidated. Scottish business people were learning that Thatcher's brave new business world which they had greeted so warmly was a chilly, rather frightening place.

The most offensive of these takeovers came in 1986 when Guinness bid for United Distillers. Ernest Saunders, the Guinness chairman, promised the moon and more. He was photographed touring Edinburgh's New Town looking for a house because, naturally, he was going to run the new company from there. He never did buy any house. He had already revealed his and the City of London's capacity for sharp practice the previous year when Guinness took over another distilling company, Arthur Bell & Co. The hostile bid came through Morgan Grenfell, who, Arthur Bell & Co thought, were their advisors. The spivvery revealed in the Distillers takeover, for which Saunders was eventually to be jailed, appalled Scottish businesses.

One of the results of all these shenanigans was that a good many Scottish business people began to think of themselves as Scottish. The subtext in this donning of national identity, never clearly articulated but understood, was that to be Scottish was to be upright and honest. The absolutely unspoken corollary was that to be English, or even British, was to be underhand and even dishonest.

The clearest manifestation of this Scottish business-Scottish Office alignment was the establishment in 1986 of Scottish Financial Enterprise, a representative body intended to promote Scottish financial companies in the wider world. The word 'integrity' and slogans such as 'Trust the Scots' featured strongly in early brochures, as did glowing accounts of Scottish history, tradition, inventiveness and culture, stressing the joy of the 'Scottish alternative' to the City of London. Laid out quite plainly was the more political goal of retaining 'the autonomy of regionally based economies'. In other words, if there was a renewed takeover threat to, say, the Royal or the Bank of Scotland, Scottish Financial Enterprise would circle the wagons in the name of Scotland's autonomy.

In this climate, Thatcher found it hard to mobilise the kind of business support she enjoyed in the South-east. Her most loyal lieutenant was James Goold, chairman of Mactaggart & Mickel, a Glasgow-based building company, who privately railed at the failure of Scottish business folk to stand up and be counted alongside the party that was reducing their tax and bureaucracy burdens. Apart from such veterans as Sir Alick Rankin, chairman of Scottish & Newcastle breweries, and Lord Weir of the Weir Group, they wouldn't even put a hand in their or the company's pocket for the party, he fumed. Goold was Thatcher's first party chairman and the only other recruits she found from business were Bill Hughes, chairman of Grampian Holdings (mainly retailing), and Jack Harvie (no relation), chairman of City-Link, a Glasgow property development firm. Harvie cracked the fund-raising problem by holding ever bigger annual dinners and charging businesses small fortunes to hear a prime ministerial speech. Hughes, who was made deputy chairman under Forsyth, brought policy advice, especially the idea of merging the Training Agency with the Scottish Development Agency to form Scottish Enterprise. But if there were more business friends of Thatcherism, they kept their heads below the parapet.

III

Then, in the mid-1980s, the political climate in Scotland turned ugly. Oil, the great drip-feed of Thatcherism, suddenly collapsed in price. Worth $40 a barrel in 1981, it was still at $30 in 1984. In April 1986 it slumped to $10. In 1985, the values of properties on which councils charged a tax – rates – were revised. There were two problems with this. First, inflation since the 1978 revaluation meant that property values, and hence the rates bills, soared. And second, the government had ducked revaluation in England so rates bills for similar properties north and south of the border were wildly out of step. This was especially true of businesses. The Tories had always resented rates because they were paid, in the main, by better-off people, i.e. Tory voters. Labour councils, they argued, racked up the rates knowing that their voters would escape lightly.

There was much citing of the widowed pensioner living alone in the former family home and having to stump up a large slice of pension, while a family of three income-earners next door paid a negligible part of their earnings. Small business owners and pensioners, the backbone of the Tory membership, arose in revolt at the 1985 Scottish Tory conference and Younger promised that something would be done.

Michael Forsyth, Stirling's MP since 1983, made out 'The Case for a Poll Tax'. Douglas Mason, a St Andrews graduate and Glenrothes Tory councillor, published a similar argument under the imprint of the Adam Smith Institute, although Smith himself had thought the idea as daft as that of a national lottery. The Cabinet which Michael Heseltine flounced out of consoled itself by approving a green paper proposing what was effectively a poll tax, but called it a community charge. It would spread local taxes over many more people, especially Labour voters, and would therefore make councils more prudent and drive local taxes downwards. Thatcher told the Scots Tories at their 1987 conference that the community charge had become law and would be brought in next year. They all cheered.

There were problems, first with the flat rate; everyone paid the same regardless of income (the government ignoring the Adam Smith Institute's advice to link it to welfare payments). Labour and the SNP compared the duke in a castle and a pensioner in a single-room flat. Worse, a duke (Westminster) did the same, found it frightfully unfair and paid all his employees' taxes himself. Second, it hit Scotland a year ahead of England, giving Nationalist rhetoric its head – Scots were being used as guinea-pigs and/or test-beds for crackpot ideology, and so on.

It was soon clear that people were going to all sorts of lengths to avoid registering for it, including dropping off electoral rolls. The SNP, languishing since the 1979 débâcle, roused itself to campaign for non-payment under the slogan 'Can't pay, won't pay'. Left-wing activists came close to forcing Labour's leaders to do likewise. Labour councils were caught between having to collect a tax they opposed or cut services because of reduced revenue. This was what the poll tax was supposed to do, of course, but the intervening stage, the warrant sale or enforced auction by sheriff's officers of non-essential household items, was a gift to the rebels. Preventing these Victorian barbarities became the province of a revolutionary left with a distinct Sherwood Forest tinge. Militant was a faction in need of a charisma transplant, but its Scottish leader, Tommy Sheridan, accumulated a folk-hero status which could only grow when in 1988 he went to Saughton jail, and the folk of Easterhouse put him on the Council.

With Europe, the poll tax would seal Thatcher's fate, but the effect in Scotland was that the Tories became indelibly stamped with the thing. Thatcher had begun her reign remarking that 'the Scots invented Thatcherism

long before I was thought of,' a reference to Adam Smith. Her own verdict on her impact on Scotland, contained in a chapter subheading in her autobiography *The Downing Street Years*, is succinctly apt: 'Thatcherism rebuffed.' Indeed, whatever credit she might have received from Scotland was all undone by this folly. And a new battle cry emerged: if Scotland had had a democratically elected parliament, Scotland would never have had the poll tax.

IV

Younger's managerial, hand-on-the-brake style essentially finessed policies devised elsewhere. He replaced Michael Heseltine at Defence after the Westland affair, and emollience gave way to intellect in the shape of Malcolm Rifkind. Rifkind was a sharp performer and his exchanges with the equally talented Donald Dewar made Scottish debates a class act which attracted the connoisseurs in a Commons more and more resembling a bear-pit. Thatcher had hopes that the advocate from middle-class Edinburgh would toe her line and as he pressed unapologetically ahead with the poll tax and privatisation, she was pleased. He was 'the best Secretary of State ever,' she cooed, like Miss Jean Brodie on Giotto. He was her favourite, but not for long. He had been a devolver, and would hint wistfully at federalism, gaining little sympathy from those who thought he'd ratted, and as time went on, less from the boss:

> No one could doubt his intellect or his grasp of ideas. Unfortunately he was as sensitive and highly strung as he was eloquent. His judgement was erratic and his behaviour unpredictable.

A catastrophic election in June 1987 didn't help. Despite – perhaps because of – an invasion of yuppy Tories eager to 'turn Scotland around', the party lost only 4.4 per cent of its vote but, thanks to tactical voting, more than half its seats. To invigilate this uncertain soul, Thatcher in 1989 gave him Michael Forsyth as a junior minister. As an Adam Smith acolyte, Forsyth had once played around theoretically with floating the pound Scots. Put in charge of health and education, the arch-loyalist carried the handbag into battle like a

Figure 7.5 The poll tax rebellion: 'Proles apart'. (opposite)
Cartoon by 'Macdonald' in *Radical Scotland*.
The sheer unfairness of the tax linked opponents – from the Duke of Westminster, who personally paid the bills of the workers on his vast Highland estate, to over a million who refused to pay at all. The backlog was simply beyond the resources of the sheriff's officers to clear up. Unfortunately, enough people dropped off the electoral rolls to help the Tories to win at least two Scottish seats in 1992. Mrs Thatcher claimed the credit. The besom! This cartoon on the poll tax was actually by a moonlighting Andrew Marr, who would graduate remarkably rapidly from *Scotsman* scribe to editor of *The Independent*.

Figure 7.6 Mikhail Gorbachev becomes leader of the Soviet Union, in Edinburgh. Rifkind and Younger in tow, 1985.
Photograph provided by *The Herald*.
This extraordinary coincidence had far-reaching implications for world history. Within five years *perestroika* and *glasnost* would destroy the Soviet Union and end the Cold War, ushering in a wave of nationalism which embarrassed rather than exhilarated.

medieval knight. He brought the market to the National Health Service to make it more efficient – he had already been a lobbyist in that cause – and berated the British Medical Association, once the Tory Party at the bedside, as the 'doctors' trade union'. Invoking parent power in education, he was unique in insisting on his own agenda instead of playing along with that of the educational establishment. Forsyth cleaved forwards, introducing elected school boards, slashing away at the teaching unions and local authorities and in

Figure 7.7 'Ad Nauseam'. (opposite)
Cartoon in *Radical Scotland*.
Among the joys of *Radical Scotland* were its cartoons. The politic *savant*, Andrew Marr, moonlighted for Alan Lawson as 'Macdonald' – showing an almost alarmingly broad range of cartoon styles – and so too did Francis Boyle. This one reflects on the problem of projecting the otherwise below-sea-level profile of the Scottish Office, which didn't even come alive to the kiss of life administered by that master of the black arts, Michael Forsyth.

Figure 7.8 The Piper Alpha disaster, 6 July 1988.
Photograph provided by *The Herald*.
No fewer than 129 oil rig workers were burned to death, suffocated or drowned in an accident – on an elderly, poorly maintained production platform which showed the price of 'the political economy of speed' in cashing in on the North Sea.

general making everyone suspect (quite rightly) that he wanted to take schools out of council control.

Rifkind's industry ought to have convinced. It was he, not Thatcher, who insisted on privatising the Hydro Board, he who converted the Scottish Development Agency and the Highlands and Islands Development Board to Scottish Enterprise and Highlands and Islands Enterprise, bringing in private business to curb horrid interventionism. But it was not enough. Rifkind kept blocking Forsyth's school board plans. So – after allowing a fairly public conspiracy against Rifkind by her younger allies – she ignored his opposition and gave the Scottish Tory chairmanship to Forsyth. Not just Rifkind but the party establishment was appalled. Writing from the fortress of Edinburgh's

New Club, one grandee noted: 'To the scalps of Galtieri and Scargill, Margaret Thatcher can now add that of the Scottish Conservative Party.'

Forsyth cleared out the genteely decayed from the party's Edinburgh headquarters and installed his own young Turks. But to the members, who adored Thatcher but not the -ism bit, these were beings from another planet, and they wanted the aliens and Forsyth taken away. Faced with an unprecedented revolt (even George Younger told her that Forsyth would have to go), she replaced him in the chairmanship by Lord Sanderson, an old-school Scottish Tory, but characteristically, she handbagged Rifkind by promoting Forsyth and making it clear in a letter which of the two would have her ear in the future.

This schism threatened to destabilise the Scottish Office and the Tory Party, but only briefly. The poll tax ignited civil disobedience and caused a major riot in England, and Thatcher went ballistic over Europe. Six weeks later the Tories swept her away and elected John Major, who immediately shunted Rifkind off

Figure 7.9 Lockerbie, 22 December 1988.
Photograph provided by *The Herald*.
Just before Christmas 1988 Pan Am Flight 103 was blown up over Lockerbie; 229 died, including several townspeople. It took over ten years to bring the two Libyans accused of the bombing to trial, but eventually, through a scheme worked out by Professor Robert Black of Edinburgh University, the Dutch air force base of Zeist became for the purpose a small bit of overseas Scotland, where the Libyans stood trial before an international panel of judges, but under Scots law and with a Scots judge presiding.

to Transport and, after the 1992 election, sent Forsyth to the Home Office. Ian Lang, privately witty, publicly proper but oh-so-languid, became Scottish Secretary and mender-in-chief of broken fences, and reverted to Younger's managerial Toryism.

All Thatcher's would-be successors promised to replace the poll tax with something else. Lang reintroduced the rates on a banded scale with rebates for single householders. His time in office was marked by two things: local government reform, which helpfully, if unintentionally, paved the way towards a Scottish parliament; and procedural change, which only demonstrated the limits to accommodating an awkward national minority. After the 1992 election he dismantled the two tiers of regional and district local government and substituted a single tier of all-purpose authorities. Labour councillors protested, the public was indifferent, and the Labour élite saw itself rid of two headaches – councils which had become mired in sleaze, and accusations that devolution would add yet another tier of bureaucrats.

V

To counter the returning tide of nationalism and demand for constitutional change, Major had promised that after the 1992 election he would 'take stock' of the constitutional situation; if the Tories lost so many Scottish seats that they could not staff the Scottish Office 'Devolution would have become inevitable, and I would have had to introduce it.' His party not only held all its seats, in two cases thanks to poll-tax dropouts, but regained Kincardine and Deeside, lost at a 1991 by-election. No crowds jangling keys turned up outside the Scottish Office, and 'taking stock' proved undramatic; the Scottish grand committee, a forum attended only by the seventy-two Scottish MPs where they could debate, but not decide, issues, could now question ministers who were not Scottish MPs and was sent to tour Scotland. Major turned up to one such meeting in Dumfries and a very jolly Burns Supper was held in the evening. Elsewhere his government was confronted with a sheep's stomachful of rebellion and distrust. Over the pound (which promptly fell out of the Exchange Rate Mechanism – ERM), over Europe (She was back and She was angry) and over the railways (flogged off at a third of their value) was poured a sticky blanquette of sleaze.

CHAPTER EIGHT

Referendum to Convention

This has always worried me about Scotland: the lack of means . . . In general, only two courses are perceived. One is the ultra-correct suit-and-tie Westminster approach through the appropriate democratic channels. The results of immaculately conducted polls or elections or petitions are presented with a little bow and the payment of the exact sum in stamp duty. . . . What do the Scots do, however, if they are rewarded with an invitation to piss off and shut up?

Neal Ascherson, 1979

What if that other single voice we all know so well responds by saying, 'We say No and We are the State.' Well, We say Yes and We are the People.

Canon Kenyon Wright, 1988

I

While 1 March 1979 was a blow to a far-from-formed nationalism and stunned home rule political agitation, it provoked a remarkable cultural reaction. The 1970s hadn't been without cultural achievement, notably John McGrath's ceilidh polemic *The Cheviot, the Stag and the Black, Black Oil* but the decade seemed fallow after the thrills of the 1960s. Not altogether so, for folk-song continued on its merrily anarchic way and reached a generation not too old to have been battered by the traumas of the 1970s.

Had the Scots, after overdoing Presbyterian seriousness and finding there wasn't much joy in that, decided to get to the heart of the matter through a good throatful and a joke? The same – sometimes more serious but usually just as alcoholic – went for language, other forms of music, the theatre, visual arts and literature. Interest in Gaelic was helped by the establishment of Sabhal Mor Ostaig, a language and culture centre on Skye, by Sir Ian Noble, an Edinburgh merchant banker who had done well out of oil. Interest picked up in the Scots language (helped by a superb BBC television adaptation of Lewis Grassic Gibbon's classic evocation of the 'speak' of the Mearns, *A Scots Quair*). The folk and the Gaelic revival led on to a Highland effusion of young bands such as Runrig, Wolfstone and Capercaillie, energetically amalgamating traditional and rock music to give Scottish youth their own Scottish rhythms. Moira Anderson could never have got tens of thousands of teenagers dancing and singing to 'Loch Lomond', but Runrig did.

Scottish theatre – too often repertory standards plus a bit of Barrie and Bridie – searched the country's dramatic potential. Glasgow's Citizens under Giles Havergal, who arrived there in 1969, had a determinedly egalitarian and community-based outlook; Edinburgh's Traverse, begun in the 1960s and

Figure 8.1
(left and opposite)
Political rock.
Photographs
provided by *The
Herald*.
The Proclaimers,
Runrig: Scottish
pop music was a
far Hue and Cry
from the Rollers,
and perhaps an
indication that
Scottish (like
Welsh) rock was
seriously
off-message as
far as Tin Pan
Alley was
concerned. But
did it influence
yoof, who might
have been
pro-SNP but
were even more
pro-apathy?

previously rather self-consciously international, looked hard at questions of local and national identity under the direction of Chris Parr, while the Lyceum thought about becoming a Scottish national theatre. Plays such as Bill Bryden's *Willie Rough*, John Byrne's *Slab Boys* trilogy, *The Hardman* by Tom McGrath and Jimmy Boyle, and Tony Roper's *The Steamie* began poking around in shipyards and factories, and up and down tenement closes. History, too, came under the lamp, notably in Liz Lochhead's *Mary Queen of Scots Got Her Head Chopped Off*, not as costume drama but an attempt to answer MacDiarmid's demand 'Hoo d'ye think we've got/From there to here?'

Visual artists exploded with activity as though 1979 had bitten their collective bum. They were already far from the London mainstream in being figurative. Scots art schools still unrepentantly followed the style of Beckmann or Dix: a new, but more confident Weimar. Peter Howson depicted the 'walking wounded' of the west of Scotland working class; Ken Currie was as political as Diego Rivera in his panoramas of militant workers and industrial decline; Keith McIntyre put rural change under the microscope; while John Bellany mined the hard religious rock of his east coast fisherfolk childhood. Kate Whiteford found new ways to bring Celtic and Pictish symbols into modern life, while Gwen Hardie's figurative skills interpreted a Scottish view of universal obsessions: religion, life and death. These and other artists were all put on show at the 1986 opening exhibition, 'The Vigorous Imagination', of Edinburgh's new Scottish National Gallery of Modern Art. For once, the title was not hype.

Writers seemed similarly affected. Before then, Scotland's most renowned living novelist, Muriel Spark, having damningly conveyed a smothering Edinbourgeoisie in *The Prime of Miss Jean Brodie*, had exiled herself to Italy. Understandably. As Iain Crichton Smith wrote, the reverse journey was:

> like shifting
> from a warm flat
> to a lonely castle
> hissing with ghosts.

Spark had a European dimension rare among English writers. So too had Allan Massie, though he was leery of the future and even more of home rule – though eloquent about it. His ghosts, unconfined to Scotland, hissed like deflating empires. The publication of Alasdair Gray's *Lanark* in 1982 was more than a literary event. 'Unblocked' by 1979, this hybrid of a book, in which fantasy of a George MacDonald sort coexisted with science fiction and grim Glasgow realism, captured the extent to which Scottish society was becoming chronically split between the affluent and the excluded. In a horribly Swiftian way, the poor lose their human characteristics, become 'dragons' and are processed into food. Concerns about deindustrialisation, nuclear destruction and crises in Scottish family and social life, looping through a 'conjectural history' of the post-war years, jangled as many nerves as *Sartor Resartus* had done 150 years earlier. Like Carlyle and MacDiarmid, Gray borrowed. Unapologetically. From the Canadian poet Dennis Lee came a motto for the decade: 'Work as if you were living in the early days of a better nation.' Many said: this is us.

II

This artistic resistance had parallels to Irish developments after a similar set-back, the death of Parnell in 1891. The shift to cultural agitation which came with the Gaelic League in 1893 had its parallels in Scottish historical and literary scholarship – not least with several big collaborative projects like *The New History of Scotland* and *The History of Scottish Literature*. In some ways this was a reaction to the successful challenge the Welsh mounted to the government's attempt to deny them the Welsh-medium television channel promised by the Annan Committee on Broadcasting. If S4C had enabled the Welsh to recover some cultural self-esteem from the appalling setback of 1 March 1979 when they voted four to one against an Assembly, the argument ran, could the Scots not attempt something similar?

The crossovers between culture and politics were, initially, few. The Traverse Theatre did run a series called Traverse Trials, in which opposing lawyers and politicians such as Malcolm Rifkind and John Smith debated topical matters, but it did not cause the box office to work overtime. One of your authors recalls visiting the Keith Folk Festival, a three-day bacchanalia, in the early 1980s and finding the Labour MP, Norman Buchan, huddled in a shop doorway listening intently as a woman sang him a Hebridean ballad. But he and his wife Janey were lone hooverers of Scottish culture in the Labour movement, regarded as eccentric for their pains, as indeed was Donald Dewar for liking books and paintings. Most SNPers, ostensible champions of Scottish culture, tended to take an essentially instrumental view of it, being interested only in such things as could be used to demonstrate how horrid England was to Scotland.

Indeed, in the 1980s, there was no *structure* to Scottish cultural identity, only a series of works in progress. An attempt was made in 1981 to establish a Scottish National Theatre under Ewan Hooper and later Tom Fleming. Their performances got critical acclaim, not audiences. When they revived Lindsay's *Thrie Estates* in 1991, the superb pageant got packed houses, but was only a last-minute addition to the Edinburgh Festival and their last outing. Were there any direct political implications to this cultural activity? In the 1980s 'God Save the Queen' was displaced as a national anthem by the dirge-like 'Flower of Scotland', written by Roy Williamson of The Corries in the 1970s, but the

Borderers, farmers and Edinburgh middle-class crowd bawling it at Murrayfield rugby internationals were not about to go out and vote SNP.

And yet, something political did emerge. The Tories missed it, not just because Thatcher was as philistine as she was humourless, and because a lot of it was socialist. There were the usual clashes over funding, the Tories seeing arts grants as they did industrial subsidy; if something needed taxpayers' cash to survive, then survive it shouldn't. What escaped them was that the condition of Scotland was actually running in a post-industrial direction, in which arts funding was a means of pump-priming effective enterprise. If something was to be done, then it had to be generated from within Scottish society and not look south for (much) cash or recognition. Nor would protest or rhetoric work.

The most remarkable manifestation of this new 'self-help-plus-the-state' philosophy was the revival of Glasgow. This started with some big, expensive projects, particularly the Glasgow Eastern Area Renewal scheme (GEAR) which built privately owned houses and business parks across what had been Jimmy Maxton's Bridgeton, between 1976 and 1987. Though lavishly funded with public money, Thatcher received no credit for it. When she visited in 1986, she stopped to talk to a crowd and asked a small child which of the local schools she attended. A woman screamed at her: 'Nane! You've shut them all doon!'

In 1984, Glasgow Council, under Michael Kelly, a young and energetic Lord Provost, came up with the 'Glasgow's Miles Better' marketing campaign complete with Roger Hargreaves' Mr Happy. The bad old past was gone, and Glasgow was excitingly different – inviting 'Is that a fact?' But along with New York's Big Apple and 'I love New York' campaigns, this turned out to be the world's top city rebranding. Neither was it just a slogan. Even habitual political opponents – Tory business people and Labour councillors – cooperated. Lord MacFarlane of Bearsden, head of the MacFarlane Group, took the chair of Glasgow Action, a private/public sector organisation which aimed, somewhat over-ambitiously, to revitalise the city's entire economy. But a lot was achieved: the opening of a gallery to house Sir William Burrell's priceless art collection, the building of a concert hall, a big new exhibition centre on one ex-dock, and perhaps most symbolic of all, a garden festival in 1988 on another. The cultural renaissance pitched in as well, with the launch of the annual Mayfest arts jamboree (and plentiful aggro from the 'Workers' City' group, often more interesting than the mainstream programme), and in 1990 Glasgow got to be European City of Culture. Not bad work inside six years.

III

And it was this non-sectarian, community-effort type of activity which was eventually to lead to the Scottish parliament we have today. Culture had a hand.

In early 1987 the BBC ran a six-part series, *Scotland 2000*, which surveyed the excitements, and more or less assumed that constitutional change would be the next step – though the Anglo-Scot Director-General Alistair Milne, who had sanctioned it, was fired as it was being made. It was from the fringes of politics that the movement for a Scottish poetry library came, and out of this agitation, successful by 1987, activists such as Judy Steel, Joy Hendry, Billy Wolfe and Ian Barr (head of the Scottish Postal Board) became involved when the Campaign for a Scottish Assembly (CSA) started to push the notion of a Constitutional Convention. The CSA had been formed by Labour home rulers, notably Jim Boyack, who held no position of any significance in the party, and a few Nationalists who had not been too scarred by 1979. Its object was not just to keep the flame alive, but (remembering the divisions in 1979) to try and get rival politicians to warm themselves around it. It was thus the inheritor of the home rule 'movement' tendency which had vanished with John MacCormick.

Cross-party action was no more than a fond hope until the 1987 general election, when the Tories hit the disaster-in-waiting that was the poll tax. A clear anti-Tory tide swept three seats to the SNP, including Banff and Buchan where Alex Salmond was elected, six to Labour and two to the SDP/Liberal Alliance. Labour was still strongest of the opposition forces. It won the Western Isles from the SNP, ousted Gordon Wilson, the SNP leader in Dundee East, and deposed Roy Jenkins in Glasgow Hillhead. But at Westminster the Tories, thanks to southern England, still had a 102 majority.

A few back-bench Labour MPs mused on extra-parliamentary tactics: what to do if the Tories were beaten in Scotland but still ran the country. This was the 'Doomsday scenario' and one suggestion was that Scottish Labour MPs should set themselves up in Edinburgh, challenge other MPs to join them and declare themselves to be a Scottish Assembly. Dewar recoiled from this but others were not so constrained. The little platoon of the CSA had toiled doggedly away until 1987, but thereafter it appeared that the mood could be capitalised on. Cue Alan Lawson, editor of *Radical Scotland*, leftish, small-n nationalist and rude, and Jim Ross, a civil servant who had worked on the 1978 Scotland Act and now, in retirement, still wanted to see it implemented. *Radical Scotland* (it published fifty-one issues between 1983 and 1991) became the centre of a network of extra-party activism centred on self-government and Third-World liberation. It was during the working-out of a distinctive Scottish anti-apartheid view that the magazine's participants were impressed by one churchman, Canon Kenyon Wright of the then Scottish Council of Churches, later to play a key role in the scheme Ross and Lawson were floating – a Constitutional Convention.

They changed the Dáil-like Constituent Assembly scheme into a meeting of politicians and other representative Scottish interests working, cross-party, to

Figure 8.2 Marching for Doomsday.
Photograph provided by *The Herald*.
The Campaign for a Scottish Assembly sees light at last. Stephen Maxwell is under the banner, with Alan Lawson of *Radical Scotland* (in beard and furry hat), creator of the 'Doomsday Scenario' – an angry man and a great editor.

draw up an agreed blueprint for an Assembly. Both reckoned rightly that an article in *Radical Scotland* would get nowhere, but what if a group of respected Scots, preferably straddling or above the party battle, should draw up the case? The fifteen-strong committee they drew together was chaired by Professor Sir Robert Grieve, a famous regional planner and former chairman of the Highlands and Islands Development Board. The trade unions, the churches, the Liberals, the SNP, the Labour Party, voluntary organisations, universities, performers, poetry activists and small businesses were all represented on it in some way or other.

The work, which was in effect mostly done by Ross, was published in July 1988 as *A Claim of Right for Scotland*, enlisting the Claims of Right in 1689 and 1842 to add historical legitimacy. Some of its argument was contradictory. The Union was somehow a constant threat to the survival of Scottish culture, yet this was a time of 'extraordinary fertility in all fields of the Scottish arts'. Where it was on strong ground was in the case, argued with great logical power by

Ross, that Scotland had voted for an Assembly consistently from 1979 onwards but that the United Kingdom political system was incapable of delivering it.

All the institutions of Scottish government – the Scottish Office, parliamentary committees at Westminster, the Scottish Secretary and ministers – had become as bogus as *Brigadoon* because the glue which had made them genuinely Scottish *within* the British political system had melted. The glue was the party system – as long as the parties for which Scots voted had a reasonable chance of winning power at Westminster, the system would work. This, broadly speaking, had prevailed up until the 1970s but now, with the Tories down to ten Scottish seats and just 24 per cent of the Scottish vote and yet holding power in Scotland thanks to their seemingly impregnable majority in England, the system was falling apart.

The *Claim of Right* said:

In the last election, political parties [Labour, SDP/Liberal Alliance and SNP] expressing the intention of creating a Scottish Assembly won 57 per cent of the United Kingdom votes cast and 76 per cent of the Scottish votes cast. In spite of which there is currently a Prime Minister dedicated to preventing the creation of a Scottish Assembly and equipped, within the terms of the English constitution, with overwhelming powers to frustrate opposition to her aims.

It went on:

We have described a situation in which the spirit underlying the Treaty of Union has been eroded almost to the point of extinction; in which the letter of approved Scottish parliamentary procedures is no longer being honoured; in which the wishes of a massive majority of the Scottish electorate are being disregarded; and in which there is only a remote hope of a response to Scottish wishes through parliamentary action. In such a situation, one would expect to see signs of a breakdown of respect for law. They are beginning to appear.

The committee cited the mounting tide of civil disobedience against the poll tax. This forced the argument that the Constitutional Convention was the only way out of the cul-de-sac.

Such a convention had to have as much authority as possible. The *Claim* proposed various models of membership. The core was formed from the Scottish MPs, plus some element consisting of elected councillors. Around that, it suggested that the political parties might have their own representatives and perhaps that other groups – the churches, trade unions, business, voluntary groups – might participate. Ideally, it thought that the Convention should be elected, but in practice it thought this would be too difficult. What was interesting was that it hit a British sense of malaise and directly affected the English movement, Charter 88. Even metropolitan conventional wisdom, confronted with Thatcher's centralisation, made its excuses and left.

IV

The lever for movement came from within the parties which were being denied the fruits of their electoral success. Malcolm Bruce, Scottish leader of the Alliance, was enthusiastic from the beginning. Donald Dewar and Gordon Wilson of the SNP were more cautious. Dewar did not want to get Labour involved in something which might end up making meaningless gestures and creating a mood of disillusion out of which the SNP could make political capital.

But Scottish Labour was feverish. The 1987 election result had turned up the heat and started some Labour MPs using the dangerously Nationalist argument that the Tories had no mandate to run Scotland. There were some notable converts, such as Robin Cook, who blurted out on television as the results rolled in that if Labour could not win a general election, he was beginning to think that devolution was a very good idea. Cook began flirting with a new party pressure group, Scottish Labour Action, formed to replace the 'British' Labour Coordinating Committee, a traditional left-wing focus which had become moribund. Led by two very articulate speakers, Bob McLean, an Edinburgh District Council worker, and Ian Smart, a lawyer from Paisley, SLA gathered around 200 recruits and agitated for a poll tax non-payment campaign and action on home rule. Non-payment was narrowly defeated at an unruly special Labour conference in Govan town hall in September, but SLA continued to call for what McLean termed 'an all-weather strategy' – something which could be implemented regardless of how a general election panned out. Still the party's Scottish executive remained very lukewarm about the Convention.

Agonising about this over many a curry in Glasgow with Murray Elder, the party's Scottish general secretary, Dewar concluded that if the convention was limited to drawing up a devolution scheme which carried cross-party support and that task occupied the time until the next election, it could not create too many hostages. Labour, by virtue of having fifty out of the seventy-two Scottish seats and controlling most Scottish local authorities, would effectively dominate and control it. So in a speech to Stirling University students in October 1988, he committed Labour to the Convention, observing that Scottish politicians were going to have 'to live a little dangerously for a while'. He reckoned that the SNP would lose out either way. If they joined the Convention, they would be supporting a scheme which could only be implemented by a Labour government. If they did not join, they would be seen as wrecking the Scottish consensus. In this regard, the Convention was the all-weather strategy that the SLA wanted.

It was not meant to be an easy decision for Gordon Wilson. Since 1979, the SNP had been split between fundamentalists, who believed there should be no truck with anything short of independence, and gradualists, who reckoned that independence would have to start out from devolution. The idea of a Convention had been hovering about the SNP since 1979, when Isobel Lindsay, a founder member of the CSA, suggested it as a way of dealing with the divisions in the 'yes' camp during the referendum.

Wilson liked the idea. Provided the convention was elected, it would be a way of repatriating Scottish sovereignty from Westminster. So did the SNP's left-wingers, notably Jim Sillars and Alex Salmond. In 1983, the party conference threw out a motion calling for a Convention, but in 1984, with an emphasis on the elected element, it narrowly approved the idea. It was still party policy when the *Claim of Right* was published.

And then Govan burst in on Scottish politics again. Its MP, Bruce Millan, had been appointed to the European Commission, but his majority of 19 000 seemed secure enough. Not so. The SNP selected Jim Sillars, quite the most formidable platform orator and street campaigner available in Scottish politics at the time. The local Labour Party, true to tradition, picked a print union official, Bob Gillespie, whose fumbling ineptitude was pitilessly exposed in the searing spotlight of a by-election. In November 1988, Sillars won by 3500 votes. The by-election, in which non-payment of the poll tax featured strongly, exposed the impotence of Labour's fifty Scottish MPs at Westminster, labelled the 'feeble fifty' by the Nationalists. Sillars, in the post-victory euphoria, was disposed to be magnanimous and talked about ways of cooperating with Labour. But Labour was in no mood to receive any hand of friendship and Sillars, 'the great manic-depressive of Scottish politics' as Stephen Maxwell once termed him, was unpredictable. He was subject to minor personal abuse which rankled, and a disgraceful attempt by a Labour MP to persuade Scottish Television to dump his wife, Margo MacDonald, from her job as a presenter of political programmes. But, more significantly, Govan had transformed his position within the SNP.

In 1981, his impressive rallying call for civil disobedience – 'we have got to be prepared to hear the sound of cell doors clanging shut behind us' – petered out in a farcical break-in at the empty Assembly building on Edinburgh's Calton Hill. In 1982, the SNP's civil war ended, with the proscription of Sillars' soul mates in the left-wing '79 Group and the expulsion from membership of several '79ers, including Alex Salmond. After more convulsions, with Sillars on the wrong end of Wilson's battle against factionalism, he departed the scene.

Figure 8.3 Sillars Redux.
Photograph provided by *The Herald*.
Govan offered yet another surprise when, broadcasting his 'Independence in Europe' message, Jim Sillars came back in November 1988, concentrating Labour's mind wonderfully on the Constitutional Convention and then, with Alex Salmond and George Washington (John Bett) going well past it. He exited in 1992, mourning Scotland's 'ninety-minute patriots'.

He returned to active politics later in the decade riding an old hobby-horse – Europe. Inspired by Irish Senator Michael Yeats, son of the poet, his argument was that the SNP should seek to make an independent Scotland part of the European Union (EU), not remain outside it. This, he reasoned, would kill off the damaging 'separatist' accusation. EU membership would mean being part of the common market, not customs posts at Gretna Green. It would also mean Scottish commissioners, more MEPs – seats at Europe's top tables, not crumbs from them. It was exciting stuff and linked him with party veterans like Winnie Ewing, 'Madame Écosse' in the European Parliament for the Highlands and Islands since 1979.

At the 1988 conference, 'Independence in Europe' became official party policy. Thus, having felled Labour in Govan and led the SNP to the intellectual high ground, Sillars had some claim to the *de facto*, if not the *de jure*, leadership of the party. In this fortified but highly suspicious mood, he went with Wilson in January 1989 to the Edinburgh offices of the Convention of Scottish Local Authorities to meet with Dewar and Bruce to see if agreement could be reached on a plan for a Convention. *Everybody* was suspicious. What emerged was inevitably a compromise. There was agreement that the Convention could only reach agreement by consensus and no votes would be taken so that nobody would be outvoted. It was agreed that the SNP should have more seats than they were entitled to by the 1987 election results, but Labour rejected the SNP demand that once the Convention had done its work, there should be a referendum in which people could choose between the Convention plan, independence and no constitutional change. That, it seemed to Dewar, was allowing the SNP to opt out of the central point of the project – to reach cross-party agreement. Wilson seemed quite happy with the outcome, but Sillars was muttering darkly that Dewar had been too clever by half.

The next day, Wilson canvassed enough opinion in the SNP to convince him that the party would not buy the Convention, fearing that it would enter a devolution trap just when the polls and Govan suggested a breakthrough. So, despite a chorus of disapproval in the media, Sillars announced that the party would not be taking part in 'Labour's rigged Convention', and the party heavily endorsed him.

V

On 30 March, the Scottish Constitutional Convention was brought to life on the hard wooden benches in the Gothic austerity of the Church of Scotland's Assembly Hall. It was an impressive turnout – fifty-eight Labour and Liberal Democrat (as the Alliance had become) MPs, most MEPs, the top brass of the Convention of Scottish Local Authorities and the Scottish Trades Union Congress, various church high-heid-yins, and a motley crew of people from the Scottish Communists, the Scottish Greens, the Orkney and Shetland autonomy movements, some representatives of ethnic minority groups and voluntary organisations. Apart from the absent SNP (though there were quite a few Nationalists in the public galleries) and the Conservatives (who were also pressing business interests to stay out) it was as representative of Scottish society as anyone could expect.

The meeting elected by acclamation two senior politicians to act as co-chairs of the Convention – David Steel, the former Liberal and Alliance party leader, and Harry Ewing, the former Scottish Office devolution minister. Appropriately enough, a representative of Scottish civil society (which, rather than the politicians, deserved the credit for the process leading up to the meeting) outdid the politicians in producing a moment of high rhetorical drama. Canon Kenyon Wright, general secretary of the ecumenical Scottish Churches Council and

Figure 8.4 The Scottish Constitutional Convention meets at Edinburgh's Assembly Hall.
Photograph provided by *The Scotsman*.
It would meet, on and off, until 1993. The Tories and SNP refused to attend and not a lot of people noticed anyway, but it was crucial in pushing Labour further towards proportional representation. This photograph shows the first session of the Scottish Constitutional Convention in the Church of Scotland Assembly Hall on the Mound and Canon Kenyon Wright making his famous speech.

whose patient skills had earned him the job of chairing the Convention's executive committee, posed a question about the ghost at the feast, Margaret Thatcher, whose '*l'état, c'est moi*' obduracy could be the rock on which it all foundered. 'What', he asked, 'if that other single voice we all know so well responds by saying: "We say No and we are the state"? A short pause and then he pulpit-thundered: 'Well, We say Yes and We are the people.' This shocking act of defiance to such a great leader appeared on news bulletins around the world. But to the cheering gathering in the Assembly Hall, who included a beaming John Smith, then the shadow Chancellor, it was an assertion of self-belief.

The road to agreement was slow and tortuous. The Scottish Labour Party was sold proportional representation – depriving it of the prospect of running a devolved Scotland on its own. This needed the most careful wooing of trade union delegations. Proportional representation (PR) passed at the 1990 Scottish party conference by the narrowest of margins, only by persuading the electricians' union delegation that the motion did not really mean what it said. On the way, there were some genuine innovations. Women politicians from Labour, the Liberal Democrats and the SNP got together under the aegis of the STUC's women's committee and formulated the idea that half the people

Figure 8.5 Canon Kenyon Wright.
Photograph provided by *The Scotsman.*
A contemporary of John Smith at Glasgow University, he went into the Church rather than into politics and after a career as a Methodist minister in Coventry and India – where he became a canon of the ecumenical United Church of South India, he returned to Scotland as the Secretary of the Scottish Council of Churches. It was in this capacity after 1987 that he became effective and painstaking leader of the Constitutional Convention.

elected to the new parliament ought to be women. Although Dewar and a good many Labour men thought this was impractical, they dared not say so without incurring the wrath of the party womenfolk. So this proposition passed into the scheme.

And on 30 November 1990, the Scottish Constitutional Convention met in Glasgow and agreed a scheme. It could by no means be described as fully formed, but there was a significant change in language. The word 'assembly' had disappeared and been replaced by the word 'parliament'. How PR would work, and how parliament would regulate income tax to have its own tax-raising power were not spelled out either. But it would have power over large areas of Scotland's economic and social life, it would be different to Westminster, and it would reflect the political wishes of the Scottish people. In a nod towards cultural Scotland, the writer William McIlvanney spoke to the meeting. In his conclusion, he said he had only one thing to tell the politicians present: 'Hurry up!'

Indeed, as far as dealing with the political threat of Nationalism was concerned, the Convention appeared to have done the trick. In a June 1989 by-election in Glasgow Central, the SNP had high hopes of repeating the coup of Govan eight months earlier. Their candidate was Alex Neil, a close friend of Jim Sillars who had followed him out of the Labour Party and through the Scottish Labour Party into the SNP. 'The new Clydesiders' claimed the legacy of Maxton and Wheatley. The poll tax and the SNP's 'Can't pay, won't pay' campaign were still live issues, but by now the problems of indebtedness and maintaining council services had surfaced. The media tackled the SNP on whether or not they had managed to amass their promised 'army of 100 000 non-payers'. A frustrated BBC reporter asked exasperatedly: 'So it's can't say, won't say?' Labour won by 6500 votes, which in by-election terms was at least a furlong, and did equally well in November in Paisley where it held two seats comfortably enough.

VI

These latter polls were overshadowed by the fall of Margaret Thatcher, occasioned by unease over the poll tax and catalysed by a clash with her Chancellor, Nigel Lawson, and the former Foreign Secretary, Sir Geoffrey Howe, over Europe. This enabled Labour to claim to the Paisley voters that it had wounded the Tories and was on its way back to government. But there was a new Tory leader to deal with.

Many Scottish Tories breathed a private sigh of relief at Thatcher's demise. Major was a totally unknown quantity; he seemed a pleasant enough cove, didn't lecture and seemed to listen. Indeed on visits to Scotland he was received so well by the public that he convinced himself he could personally rescue the Tories and the Union. He got rid of the poll tax and set about convincing the Scots that their best bet lay with the Union and not with devolution or independence. He produced some juicy morsels to prove that Scotland was dear to his heart, such as announcing that the December 1992 summit of European government leaders would be held in Edinburgh.

Throughout the Tory years, there was always an enigma at the heart of the constitutional debate. The opinion polls maintained that the Scots wanted constitutional change. Broadly speaking, independence usually got between 25 and 30 per cent support, devolution 40–50 per cent support and the remaining minority said they liked what they had, thank you. Yet polls also found that people gave a low priority to achieving constitutional reform, well behind doing something about unemployment, the health service, education, housing and so on. For years, Malcolm Rifkind carried in his wallet a cutting from *The Scotsman* showing that more people were worried about AIDS than were interested in devolution. This lack of interest tallied with the few letters that MPs and ministers got from the public about the subject.

It was certainly true that in the first half of the Tories' eighteen years devolution aroused as much public interest as the weather in the Himalayas, to quote an unwise parallel that Neil Kinnock once used. But in the second half, it is arguable that people came to use the constitutional issue as a barometer by which they could judge how interested politicians were in Scotland. The SNP wanted devolution, Labour and the Liberal Democrats wanted devolution, so they were all interested in Scotland. The Tories did not want any assembly or parliament, so they were not interested in Scotland.

Major eventually concluded that what he needed to do was to raise the salience of the constitutional issue and turn people against major change by pointing out all the downsides – higher taxes, lower public spending, isolation and so on. The Tories' negative image would be tackled by frequent prime ministerial visits and by conveying the impression that the Tories would consider change, but only *within* the existing union. By the end of January 1992, with a general election at most five months away, this became an urgent priority. An opinion poll by ICM, *The Scotsman*'s pollsters, came out with the startling news that 50 per cent of Scots wanted independence. It made the lead item on ITN's *News at Ten* and was reported around the world. Most Scottish politicians, including some in the SNP, thought it could not be right and dismissed it as a rogue poll.

But there were a number of reasons to think that a tide of Nationalism had built up and this poll caught it at the flood. First, the previous September's SNP party conference had been a good one. Alex Salmond had taken over the leadership from Gordon Wilson a year before and projected a new youthful and dynamic image, as did the support that the SNP had gained from such popsters as Pat Kane of the duo Hue and Cry. Salmond was privately enraged when the party's leftists sprang the slogan 'Free by '93' on the public, but in fact it probably contributed to the image of a party on the move while Labour was marking time until the election. And the SNP had a new public voice, Sean Connery, whose dishtinctive shyllables were to be heard on its party political broadcasts. If Hollywood's greatest backed the SNP, surely it could not fail?

Second, in November, the Tories lost a seat, Kincardine and Deeside, to the Liberal Democrats, who immediately hailed the result as a step towards home rule. It was nothing of the kind; the prosperous electorate voted for a candidate, Nicol Stephen, who had been nursing the seat for years and who campaigned on every broken pavement issue he could find. Nevertheless, the effect was to reduce the Scottish Tories to nine seats, fewer than the Liberal Democrats which put them in third place in terms of parliamentary rankings in Scottish politics. It was a position of unparalleled weakness for a governing party.

Third, in January, the now-privatised British Steel Corporation announced the closure of the Ravenscraig steelworks at Motherwell. It had only arrived there by political decision and it departed when its political guarantee, wrung out of a grudging steel corporation by Malcolm Rifkind and Margaret Thatcher (who felt she owed the steelworkers for keeping going during the miners' strike) in 1987, finally ran out. Nevertheless, it was seen as heralding the final death of Scotland's traditional industries and Ian Lang could only say how sorry he was. To be honest, there was nothing he could have done, but there was still an unreasonable expectation that he should have done something.

Fourth, in mid-January, *The Scotsman* staged a remarkable public debate between the four party leaders. Only Donald Dewar was reluctant to appear. He thought it was a waste of time, as most people would have better things to do on a Saturday night than listen to a load of politicians. He was wrong. *The Scotsman* had three times more takers than the 2500 tickets which were available. This queue formed mainly because SNP members rushed to get as many seats as they could, which became obvious when the debate began. Salmond was well prepared, spoke well and was constantly cheered. Dewar was ill prepared, hesitant and constantly booed. Malcolm Bruce argued cleverly but did not have the support in the hall to make an impact. Lang ignored the jeering and concentrated on speaking to the audience outside the hall. The whole two and half hours were broadcast live on radio by BBC Scotland. It was rumbustious, unpredictable, old-time political theatre, the sort of thing which has probably not been heard since Gladstone's Midlothian campaign. Who won the debate did not matter; the effect was to tell the electorate that the constitutional debate was up, running and important.

Fifth, at the end of January and just a few days before ICM pollsters started

Figure 8.6 The party leaders clash at the Usher Hall.
Photograph provided by *The Scotsman*.
The debate was arranged by *The Scotsman*. Alex Salmond was reckoned to have won, but it didn't do his party much good in an election in which media enthusiasm for home rule wasn't reflected in the vote.

work, *The Sun* newspaper announced it was backing the SNP and independence. On the background of a St Andrew's cross, its front page blared: 'Arise and be a Nation Again'. This was no more than a crude calculation by *The Sun* management that such a move would help them gain circulation in their battle for readers against the Labour-supporting *Daily Record*. The Nationalist stance extended only to the newspaper's Scottish editions but the policy shift, the first time that the SNP had ever had the overt support of a major newspaper, was extensively reported on and debated by the rest of the Scottish media.

Even if the 50 per cent support for independence reported by *The Scotsman* was not to be believed (the figure fell back sharply thereafter), there was good reason to think that some sort of Nationalist surge was happening. So over the next few weeks, John Major and a string of other Tory ministers filled seats on flights to and from Scotland, making a barrage of speeches stressing the benefits of the Union and the disasters that lay in store if it was ever abandoned.

VII

If all this signalled that Scotland was heading towards a great constitutional crunch, there were economic and social movements that said otherwise. The Glasgow renaissance we have met, but the City of Culture and the Merchant City were at a far remove from the council schemes which became an ever more intractable social problem. Purchase of the better houses by their tenants meant that unpopular estates became areas of multiple social deprivation with a swelling drug problem, almost a modern parallel to Nicoll Jarvie and Rob Roy in the eighteenth century. It was the city's burgeoning crime writing, led by William McIlvanney, which also worried about the evolution of a secret state and deep shifts in Scottish society. The religious divide was less pronounced, as working-class Protestantism retreated into an Orange ghetto; and after creeping up on the Church of Scotland, decade after decade, the Catholic Church started to slip back, just after receiving, in 1982, the imprimatur of a papal visit. After a spasm of gang violence in the 1960s and 1970s, social life became less violent, not least because of the liberalisation of the licensing laws in 1976. The Scottish football fan, once a byword for drunken horseplay, if not worse, cleaned up his act and by 1983 was being recognised as a somewhat zany guarantor of fair play by – let's face it – not very good national teams. This contrasted with the behaviour of English fans, especially after the Falklands War. As the monarchy sagged in public esteem, the Scots showed a dignified distancing, both from the tabloids and the institution itself. Scots prided themselves on giving more to charity and being less showy with their wealth.

All of these developments were validated and reinforced by attitude polls which seemed to show Scottish public opinion steadily diverging from UK norms. But how valid was this? Football in Scotland was actually more commercialised, if assessed on expenditure per head of population, than in England. Nothing said 'yuppy' louder than the lifestyle of the winners in Glasgow's Merchant City. Surveys showed an alarming ignorance of Scottish history and culture among schoolchildren.

The 1992 election result seemed to indicate that the media and chattering classes' obsession with devolution and independence was just that, a media and chattering classes' obsession. Misled perhaps by the opinion polls, the pundits' predicted wipeout of the Tories just did not happen. The Tories pretended afterwards that they knew all along that it would be quite alright on polling day. Actually, they did not. Party staff at headquarters conducted a private sweepstake on the number of seats they would have when the polls closed. Most enthusiasm was for the tickets which said six seats or less.

Economic factors played a part. The Scottish economy had revived and the Tories' warnings that Labour would drop a tax bombshell on those who were profiting from it hit home, especially in the North-east where they won back Aberdeen South and Kincardine and Deeside and nearly evicted Malcolm Bruce from Gordon. Elsewhere, Major's 'Save the Union' message, tooted to mystified London and scornful Scots journalists, appeared to have worked. The SNP's John Swinney, standing in Tayside North, initially thought that the maverick Union Jack campaign by the Tory MP, Bill Walker, was so bizarre it could be ignored. But the closer it got to polling day, the more he noted people telling him that they could not risk the Union by voting Nationalist, even though they disliked the Tories and Walker in particular. Other parties noted the same thing happening in other Tory seats. On Friday, 10 April 1992, Scots woke up to find that the only thing which had changed was the size of the Tories' British majority, reduced to twenty-one. In Scotland, they still had eleven seats. It was enough to rule, uneasily perhaps, but enough to rule.

CHAPTER NINE

The Settled Will?

But I have dreamed a dreary dream,
Beyond the Isle of Skye;
I saw a dead man win a fight,
And I think that man was I

'The Battle of Otterburn'

I

There were two reactions to the election result. The Tories were surprised and delighted. There was a certain amount of crowing, but not too much. Ian Lang, encouraged by one newspaper columnist to invite all the media pundits to a dinner consisting of such dishes as humble pie and egg-on-face, politely declined, gent that he was. In fact, he had a bit of a problem. The manifesto, constructed with the subconscious thought that it was unlikely to be implemented, was thin and mostly consisted of phrases of the 'we will continue . . .' type. They promised only one major piece of Scottish legislation, the new council system. The much hinted-at 'taking stock' would not entail legislation.

The second reaction was of deflation and disillusion. The fizz had gone from the ginger, deep blue skies turned pallid and grey. William McIlvanney wrote: 'Most of us wore gloom like some uniform from Orwell's *1984*.' The morning after polling day, *The Scotsman* received a mobile phone call from two men, apparently quite sane, who had been so upset by the result that they had driven to Carlisle, scaled its castle walls with the aid of a ladder, and hoisted a St Andrew's flag to take the castle in the name of Scotland. Jim Sillars, who lost his Govan seat, raged that the Scots were 'ninety-minute patriots'. He went back to his business interests, lecturing Scotland in general and Alex Salmond in particular from his column in *The Sun*.

The dismay was not imaginary. During the election, one of the big life assurance companies had said, in response to Tory cajoling, that if there was a Scottish parliament it would have to review its position, implying that it would move south of the border. Afterwards, its directors thought that the impact of this on staff morale had been so bad and that employees had been so disappointed by the election result, that the company would never again comment on the issue.

The truth was more prosaic. Non-Tory voters had been led by the media and the opinion polls to expect change. The dashing of that expectation led to the adverse reaction. The combination of the Tories' 'tax bombshell' campaign – aimed at John Smith, the failure of Neil Kinnock to project a competent image, and poll tax defections bolstered the Tory vote by just enough to enable them to hold their ground. The unionist campaign was only important at the margins.

By any yardstick, the Tories with 26 per cent of the Scottish vote and just eleven of seventy-two seats had been rejected by Scottish voters. But the fact of their recovery, however slight, was such a shock that it seemed to legitimate their right to run Scotland. Certainly, the opposition reacted in that way. Donald Dewar said that the government should hold a multi-option referendum – a choice between independence, devolution and the status quo, an SNP policy that he had previously rejected, but there was no activity to back this up. Malcolm Bruce, holding his seat only after a recount, eventually opted for Westminster. Alex Salmond, hoist by the petard of 'free by '93', was in no position to claim anything.

Yet Labour's position was in no doubt. When John Smith replaced Neil Kinnock, he made it plain that achieving a Scottish parliament was 'unfinished business'. As a devolution minister in the last Labour government and as an enthusiast for the Constitutional Convention, this meant a firm commitment to the cause. At Westminster the Conservative British nationalists decided that John Major's mild pro-Europeanness was too extreme for them and the Tories began, fatally, to divide over the Maastricht Treaty. Among the rebels was Teddy Taylor, transplanted to Southend where his devotional Unionism flickered among south-eastern patriots he liked less than he should have. A century earlier, he would have been fighting for queen, country and Union flag on some imperial frontier – though his reverence for Bob Marley was less classifiable.

Other groups began to rally support behind the home rule cause: disparate roots, different cast lists but a similar theme. 'Common Cause' gathered thinkers and writers and tried to unite politicians. 'Democracy for Scotland', a more vagrant lot associated with environmental activity, mounted a vigil outside the gates of the empty Assembly on Calton Hill. Scotland United boasted Labour and Liberal Democrat politicians and some SNP-supporting artists and musicians. On the Sunday after polling day, it filled Glasgow's George Square with about 5000 people, a remarkable turnout given the haste with which the event was put on. Rather more significantly, around 25000 people marched for democracy during the European summit in Edinburgh that December, the biggest such march anyone could remember seeing in the capital.

If these were optimistic signs, there was plenty to be gloomy about. Donald

Figure 9.1 Europe in Edinburgh: 'A' the bairns o' Adam'.
Photograph provided by *The Scotsman*.

After his victory in April John Major thought he could afford to be generous, and persuaded the EU to stage one of its less conclusive summits in Edinburgh. Then he slammed into the September Black Friday devaluation crisis. The meeting of the EU heads of government in December 1992 was used as the excuse for a mini-festival and a massive demonstration for home rule, and on a cold winter Saturday 25 000 turned out to watch home rule leaders squabble and Hamish Henderson sing them back to unity. The bickering of the politicians was healed by his eloquence.

Dewar said that Labour would have nothing to do with Scotland United as the Nationalists would turn it against them. Things got even worse when SNP MPs voted with the Tories against a Labour amendment to the Maastricht Treaty bill – the carrot was more Scottish representatives on Europe's new Committee of the Regions – and Salmond had his knuckles rapped hard by his party. While Salmond was personally inclined towards cross-party cooperation, this episode left him tied to a harder independence position. The Liberal Democrats were also uneasy about cooperation; many thought that the Constitutional Convention had identified them too much with Labour, and lost votes.

II

It was a time to reassess positions and look back over recent history, not least because so little of the country's industry was any longer rooted in the past. By 1992 shipyards were down to under half a dozen, deep coal mines to two – Longannet in Fife and doomed Monktonhall in Midlothian – and textile-makers were painfully aware of how far jobs and production had slumped. In their place the great growth areas were finance, up from 7 to 15 per cent of employment between 1980 and 1998, and the electronics of Silicon Glen, which now accounted for over 40 per cent of Scotland's exports. Finance was deeply dependent on the whims of the City of London and the blind hunger for high returns of corporate shareholders, while the Scottish electronics industry was essentially a 'screwdriver' operation, dependent on imported components for all but 5 per cent of its production.

Nevertheless Scotland was now so deeply implicated in these international operations that its business cycle had now become distinctive from that of the South. Where once if the South-east sneezed, the North caught a cold, now Scotland merely sniffled. If the British boom of 1988 was merely a ripple north of the border, so the slump of 1990–2 was a dip in Scotland. That too appeared to be true in politics. While the sudden exit of sterling from the European Exchange Rate Mechanism lethally injured the Conservatives, their claims to economic competence and ultimately to their tenure of power, this opportunity passed unnoticed among Scottish politicians. The Convention slumbered on.

The opposition denounced the government's 'taking stock' proposals as totally inadequate, and enjoyed the new facilities for further denunciation of Tory policies and each other. Ian Lang might well have thought it was all working quite satisfactorily when, a Major loyalist in the leadership contest of 1994, he was given Trade and Industry as a reward. A less plausible Majorite, Michael Forsyth came back from obscurity at the Home Office to be Scottish Secretary. For the *Daily Record* the nightmare had returned and the public sector geared itself up to relive all the battles it had fought with Forsyth as a junior minister.

Figure 9.2 Ian Lang with crushed head . . .
Photograph provided by *The Scotsman*.
The penultimate Tory Secretary of State and knight of the rueful countenance contemplates a memento mori for his party, on the occasion of a visit by French artists in 1995.

But this was a new Forsyth, who went about being nice to people. Not just nice but very, very nice. Problems in the health service? He hired more doctors. Problems in schools? He gave teachers more time to implement curriculum changes. Almost comically, the Scottish Trades Union Congress, astounded that he had agreed to meet them, turned up with a list of about twenty demands. Forsyth agreed to almost all of them and seduced a dazed Campbell Christie, the STUC general secretary, into appearing at a joint press conference to discuss the new concord. Margaret? Margaret who?

Indeed Forsyth, like Lang and Rifkind before him, went back to the devolution files, partly to find out the costs of devolution to use as ammunition against Labour, but also to see if there was any way that Scotland could be given self-government. He concluded, like Lang and Rifkind, that there was no way that meaningful self-government could be granted without damaging the

Union. Instead, he could use his considerable powers as Scottish Secretary to sort out as many problems as possible. The Union would be shown to work by delivering.

Forsyth rushed about Scotland as though his tail was on fire. Indeed his ministerial car was once nabbed speeding on the M9. Fewer were more astonished than Highlanders. A community wanted to buy a forest to create some work. They got it. Crofters were keen on owning their crofts. If these were on government-owned land, they came at bargain-basement prices. For years, Highland bodies had argued for a university, denounced by bureaucrats in Edinburgh as an expensive and damaging fantasy. Forsyth overruled them, taken with the notion of a virtual university with campuses spread all across the region, linked by its superb telecommunications. It was the same in most

Figure 9.3 Michael Forsyth back as Secretary of State.
Photograph provided by *The Herald*.
'He's back and he's happy!' After the John Major leadership battle with John Redwood in 1995 Michael Forsyth ditched his fealty to Mrs Thatcher and returned to St Andrew's House as a Major loyalist, offering sweeties to a' the bairns o' Adam. After an astonishing makeover, the New Model was anxious to compromise with his auld enemies, it seemed, on every subject but one.

Figure 9.4 'God gave the Land to . . . well . . . who?'
Photograph provided by *The Herald*.
The oldest grievance of the lot surfaced in the Major government's last years. Several particularly scandalous land sales stirred up great resentment and schemes for crofters' buyouts. In Assynt they were successful enough to bring Michael Forsyth north, offering to transfer state land to its cultivators but quiet about private landowners. It didn't do his party much good but put land reform to the head of the new parliament's agenda.

other policy areas. Civil servants either loved his decisive actions or loathed him for making them work on into the night.

If this really was Freddy Krueger's return to Elm Street, as the *Record* had shrieked, this Freddy just had treats to hand out. Where were his tricks? He had plenty but they were played with guile. A potentially alarming catalyst for an upwelling of Nationalism during this time was the attention paid to 'battles long ago' by Hollywood. A native film industry had tried hard over the years, despite meagre returns, to put contemporary Scotland on the silver screen. Films such as *Gregory's Girl* mused over the difficulties of new town youth and changing mores, *Carla's Song* portrayed Scottish internationalism and generosity towards the oppressed, while *Shallow Grave* countered cruelly that even Scotland's much-vaunted social solidarity could be splintered by instant wealth.

But in the mid-1990s Hollywood rode into town with ambitious projects like Michael Caton-Jones's *Rob Roy* and Mel Gibson's *Braveheart*, the latter an idiosyncratic interpretation of the career of William Wallace. Undeterred by the film's 'freedom' battle cry, a kilted Forsyth threw a lavish bash at Stirling Castle for Gibson and the cast, and ordered the enterprise agencies to see what they could do to bring more of this film-making to Scotland. Forsyth's most spectacular initiative reversed 'Malleus Scotorum's' greatest hit. In November 1996, he persuaded Major to prevail over the misgivings of the Queen and the Dean and Chapter of Westminster Abbey and return the Stone of Scone to Scotland. Coming on the 700th anniversary of its seizure, and just after *Braveheart*, this did the late John MacCormick's job for him. Forsyth's aim was to clad the Scottish Tories in tartan patriotism, but unlike Prince Charles's investiture at Caernarfon three decades earlier, this wasn't a strategy of symbolic unity. It was seen as a surrender. But who would pick up the banner? If the Labour Party, what sort of Labour Party?

III

In May 1994, Labour and Scotland suffered the hammer-blow of the death of John Smith. His solidity, embracing personality and enveloping gregariousness had somehow come across to people who had never met him, and meant that all Scotland was plunged into mourning: even his unrelenting Tory opponents, at their conference in Inverness when Smith died. Ian Lang wept as he paid tribute, the tears of a Scot with a private pride in another Scot's achievements. That evening, Forsyth discussed with friends who was likely to take over from Smith and commented: 'The one I fear is Tony Blair.'

And so it came to be. Blair, a telegenic leader for a television age, was elected by as clear a margin in Scotland as in the rest of the country. Straightaway, he set about putting his modernisation mantra into practice. Smith had begun the drive towards one-member-one-vote democracy but retained Clause IV's socialism, even though the commitment had long ceased to mean anything. The debate and the eventual vote punctured the myth that Scottish Labour was well to the left of Blair – with party conference and membership voting happily to get rid of it – but what did Blair really think about home rule?

In fact, the Convention had staggered back into life a year before Blair became leader. George Robertson had been appointed shadow Scottish Secretary in 1993 (Dewar had been shunted off to social security) and had started re-energising the Convention. Fortunately, he got on well with Jim Wallace, who had replaced Malcolm Bruce as the Scottish Liberal Democrat (SLD) leader,

Figure 9.5 Returning the Stone of Destiny.
Photograph provided by *The Herald*.
Spurred by the success of Mel Gibson's William Wallace epic *Braveheart* – a Hollywood
farrago which occasionally encountered the odd historical fact – politicians went
briefly ethnic in 1996. No one more so than Michael Forsyth, who persuaded his
by-then-desperate patron John Major to appease the jocks by repatriating the Stone of
Scone. The Stone itself, Land-rovered over the Tweed at Coldstream in the presence of the
diminutive Secretary of State and assorted brass hats, proved underpowered in the
charisma stakes.

Figure 9.6 The funeral of John Smith on the island of Iona, May 1994.
Photograph provided by *The Scotsman*.
Initially sceptical about devolution, Smith had piloted the luckless Scotland Act through the Commons in 1978.
As leader of the Labour Party he believed it to be 'the settled will of the people of Scotland'. It was his
'unfinished business', a quotation continually audible during the referendum campaign.

and there was a similarly good relationship between Jack McConnell, general
secretary of the Scottish Labour party, and Andy Myles, his SLD counterpart.

They tightened up the financial powers so that the parliament, like the
proposed 1978 Assembly, would get a block grant from the Treasury (essentially
the same block grant as then went to the Scottish Office) but unlike the old
Assembly plan, it could tax, or more precisely vary, up or down, the basic rate
of income tax by up to 3p. A proposal to make the parliament responsible for
the administration of social security was dropped. There remained, however,
the business of defining the proportional representation system. There were
plenty of plans. The STUC urged a 200-seat parliament which would allow for
ethnic minority representation, for balanced numbers of men and women, and
for a fully proportional system. This got a great deal of support from Labour. The
Liberal Democrats, on the other hand, wanted 145 seats. Robertson worried
that the bigger the parliament, the more difficult it would be to get the bill

through Westminster, with opponents arguing about monstrous expense. He favoured 112 seats.

Two other issues complicated the matter. One was the voting system. The Liberal Democrats wanted a pure proportional system, based on the single transferable vote in multi-member constituencies, but Labour insisted on maintaining the link between representatives and their constituencies. So they settled for the additional member system, a number of seats filled in the usual first-past-the-post way, and then some additional members elected in proportion to the share of the votes the parties got.

The other was Labour's policy that the voting system specified in the act should put parties under an obligation to field an equal number of men and women candidates. The Liberal Democrats argued this offended against the principle of freedom of voters' choice, and moreover was impractical; a party could still put all its female candidates into unwinnable seats, so defeating the object. Robertson and Wallace agreed to sideline this issue by signing a non-binding election agreement that they would jointly aim to have gender balance on their election slates. Happily, the two chairs of the parties, Rhona Brankin, Labour, and Marilyn McLaren, Liberal Democrat, were women so the ceremony struck a nice gender balance (even if the LibDems then forgot about it).

Eventually the numbers problem was brokered by a straightforward negotiation between Robertson and Wallace, conducted at the Edinburgh home of Menzies Campbell MP. They compromised on a 129-seat parliament with seventy-three constituency members and fifty-six additional members comprising seven members for each of eight electoral regions. For the Liberal Democrats this was enough to produce a broadly proportional parliament. In an adroit move, Robertson slipped this through Labour's national policy forums before they saw that a part of Labour's election manifesto had been written to accommodate another party.

This could be important for the rest of Britain as the successful operation of proportional representation would increase pressure for reform in Westminster elections. It was expected to accelerate the introduction of PR to local government elections in Scotland and, less certainly, for such elections elsewhere. The template agreed in Scotland gave the minority proponents of PR in the Welsh Labour Party a winning hand, and they adopted the Scottish scheme. Also transferred to Wales was the method Labour chose to achieve gender balance amongst its candidates – pairing constituency parties so both constituencies would jointly select a man and a woman for the two seats.

IV

But the next development threatened to derail the entire home rule scheme.

Blair insisted that the manifesto had to be capable of being legislated on at Westminster with a minimum of fuss and be immune to any future Conservative government. Neither of these conditions was met by the Scottish parliament bill, as a committee under Lord Irvine of Lairg, the shadow Lord Chancellor, rapidly discovered when it examined the scheme approved by the Convention on St Andrew's Day 1995.

Going on the experience of the 1970s, the bill could consume as much as half of the available parliamentary time, squeezing out other legislation important to Blair. If Labour's majority was, say, only about forty, it could be ambushed and amended by rebellious back-benchers and in the Conservative-dominated House of Lords. One amendment that the government could not count on defeating would be a call for a referendum. The committee could find no way past this and had to concede. Robertson kept mum, fearing that if it leaked out, a 'sell-out' campaign against a referendum would be hard to stop.

The committee, which also included Dewar and Brown, considered taxation too. Forsyth was campaigning hard on it, having snappily labelled the power to vary income tax as the 'tartan tax' and claiming Labour was planning to tax Scots more heavily than anyone else in Britain. Again the Irvine committee could not be sure that was safe from a Commons defeat, so decided that the referendum should have two questions – one on the general principle of the parliament, and a second on taxation powers. This would take the wind out of Forsyth's tartan tax sails.

When Robertson announced the referendum plan in June 1996, there was the most unholy row. The Convention co-chairs were affronted. They had not been consulted. Harry Ewing resigned. The press was enraged, partly because they had been scooped the previous day by Andrew Marr, a long-time devolution advocate who was now editor of *The Independent*, and partly because they had been told for ages that a general election verdict was a sufficient mandate. The Liberal Democrats were furious. They, like Labour's left, smelled a devolution sell-out by Blair. Labour nationalists suspected a ploy to generate a 'no' vote to the second question, thereby emasculating the parliament. John McAllion, the Dundee East MP and a nationalist, resigned from Robertson's front-bench team. Worse than that was the insult to the memory of John Smith. Had he not declared it to be the 'settled will' of the Scottish people that they should have their parliament?

But fifteen years previously Smith had come to the same conclusion as the Irvine committee. He gave an interview to Neal Ascherson and Tom Nairn in 1981, which they published in an obscure academic journal. It lay there forgotten until Lindsay Paterson, an Edinburgh University academic, rediscovered it in 1998 while compiling a book on the devolution debate, *A Diverse Assembly*. In the interview, Smith said that he thought a referendum on new plans for an

Assembly would be inevitable. He went on:

> I would urge the government to 'front-end' the referendum: let me
> explain what that would mean. Any new Labour government would of
> course confront the question of priorities in its legislative programme;
> and we would have to argue priority for a new Scottish assembly bill. Now
> it will be very hard to counter the objection that another government
> might find itself spending a disproportionate amount of time and energy
> on such a bill, only to get it rejected once more. So by far the best way
> would be to prepare a white paper with a sufficient outline of that scheme
> – not necessarily all the detail – and hold the referendum on that. This
> would be an advisory referendum, which would give the government
> solid grounds for pressing ahead.

And that was pretty much what was to happen. But first the Scottish public
and the Labour Party had to accept it. Blair came to Edinburgh the day after
the announcement. He had a meeting with newspaper editors but was unable
to win them over as they were convinced his office had leaked the plan to Marr
as a snub to them. He gave a speech at Edinburgh University but the audience
was carefully controlled to make sure that there were no unseemly eruptions.
He went on to a meeting of the Scottish Labour executive which proved
unwilling to lie down and accept the new line. Instead of the one hour he
planned to stay, he spent three hours locked in debate. Eventually the executive
voted 16–12 to accept the two-question referendum, but for Robertson the
nightmare was still to come.

The executive also agreed to consult the party membership, and the unconvinced (mainly the left and the nationalists in the party) waged a campaign to
ditch the second question. When it came to the August executive meeting,
Robertson had eighteen votes and the opponents had eighteen votes. In the
middle there were three waverers. After hours of negotiation, a frustrated
Robertson accepted a scheme proposed by Mohammed Sarwar, Labour's
candidate in Govan, that after the first two-question referendum, the taxation
power could only be activated by the Scottish parliament after a second referendum. The plan was ridiculous. Robertson knew but it was the only way to
preserve the two-question plan. After enduring a few days of derision, he
dropped the additional referendum plan.

VI

It was catastrophe time for Robertson and the Scottish Labour Party.
Robertson had hoped to put the SNP in a difficult spot – would they support

a 'yes' vote in a referendum, a question which he knew would divide them? But now they were able to laugh it off. Which referendum? they chortled. Labour had gone, in a matter of weeks, from no referendum, to a two-question referendum, to a two-part three-question referendum, to a two-question referendum. What was coming next? The Tories, whom Robertson had hoped to pin down as 'no' stalwarts, escaped equally easily.

There was a fearful lesson for home rulers from all of this. The years of debate in Scotland, the campaigning by party and cross-party groups, the hours of negotiation in the Constitutional Convention had had little effect on Westminster. It was as though its politics had become completely divorced from Scottish politics. In this atmosphere an unrealistic mind-set took root. It became assumed that what Scotland wanted Scotland would automatically get whenever a sympathetic government was elected. Scotland was the dog and when it barked, Westminster would wag its tail.

But it could not be so. Devolution could only became a fact if Westminster said so and first Westminster would want to debate it, probably endlessly. The proof of the wisdom of the Irvine committee and John Smith's much earlier judgement would be demonstrated after the election, but the lesson of this episode was that Scottish politics was still part of British politics and had to fit in with British political machinery, of both party and government, if there was to be any constitutional change affecting Scotland short of full independence.

Indeed, British politics came to the rescue of a battered Robertson and bruised Scottish Labour Party. As the election drew closer, the Tories fell into further and deeper disarray over Europe and became mired in a slough of sleaze. Against that, Blair's tightly controlled Labour Party looked ever more competent and purposeful. A Labour victory in April 1997 became a racing certainty. The only question was: how big would Blair's majority be?

CHAPTER TEN

New Dawn and Old Ghosts

who wants to be free
who has need of air

who is changing

who has a different definition
who has no definition

instance
(the right)
who wants to find out what it is
who wants to go forward

who wants to

> Tom Leonard, 'Proem', New Scottish
> Writing VII, edited by Harry Ritchie,
> Bloomsbury, 1996

Scottish 'identity' is, of course, a myth. It is a given substance only in the corporealities of persons who imagine they have it. There is nothing outside consciousness which is 'identity', though Scots may invest their individual identities in Scottish landscape or Scottish football, Scottish poetry and music, or Scottish beef cattle.

> Angus Calder, 'By the Water of Leith I Sat Down and Wept:
> Reflections on Scottish Identity', New Scottish Writing VII

I

The morning after polling day on 1 May 1997 was unlike the morning after any other general election. Labour folk couldn't believe the scale of their triumph. Candidates who had stood in no-hope seats suddenly became MPs. Jim Murphy, who had spent next to no time in true-blue Eastwood – a good try-out for a safe seat later on – discovered that those Tories were sending him to Westminster four years ahead of schedule. Even Dumfries, visited rather theatrically by Tony Blair in a squadron of helicopters on the eve of the election, fell to his charms. New Labour, targeted on middle England, won over middle Scotland too.

In the midst of the euphoria over a Tory wipeout in Scotland and Wales, more than a few Scottish Labourites quietly wondered whether it was really worth bothering with devolution. With this majority, a Labour government could do anything it liked. But the election also exposed some quiet and terribly fundamental facts. Statistically it was the Tories' worst result since 1832, but it was closer in its party implications to the split of 1846, in which Disraeli's seizure of the party for protection condemned it to the wilderness for nearly thirty years. More profound than that was the fact that part of Britain's unwritten constitution had been shredded.

The SNP in the 1970s had chipped away at the party-system bond, but the eclipse of the Tories had snapped it almost completely. Now only the Labour Party and (but much more weakly) the Liberal Democrats straddled the border. Blair had to deliver what had been promised, and fast, or the Scottish Labour Party would revolt and the Union (and half of Blair's Cabinet) would go.

Though he had no other intention: 'We say what we mean, and we mean what we say,' he told his party before the election, and while his own notions of decentralising government would have been somewhat different, he had promised that Labour would deliver the Constitutional Convention's plans within a year of taking office. Moreover, the timing was already in hand. A short bill, passed only weeks after the election, would set the polling date for early autumn, while the white paper on which the vote would be held would be drafted in parallel. The need for time to negotiate in Whitehall over the powers of the parliament and the drafting of those negotiated outcomes into the legal language of a bill meant that there would be a gap of maybe six months before the Government of Scotland bill would lie before the Commons.

Neatly – and as it turned out, fortunately – the Welsh would vote a week after the Scots. The Welsh wouldn't be overshadowed in the media by reportage of the Scottish debate, while a good result in Scotland was likely to bring them sufficiently into line to achieve the 150 per cent swing needed from 1979, and so give an aura of symmetry to devolution as a Britain-wide policy.

Then a minor miracle occurred in the fractious world of Scottish politics. Labour, the Liberal Democrats and the SNP agreed to campaign jointly for a 'yes-yes' vote. Since the Liberal Democrats had stuck with Labour in the Scottish Constitutional Convention and both parties had backed the same scheme in the 1997 general election, this element was pretty predictable. Less so was the alliance with the SNP. Many of its leaders still smarted under the 'betrayal' of the 1979 referendum. The SNP had denounced the Convention as a 'puppet parliament'. They saw the referendum as a Blair ploy to ditch devolution, and scorned it as 'rigged' because independence wasn't an option on the ballot paper. There were opponents on the Labour side – viewing the SNP as wreckers, distracting the voters from the task of ousting the Tories. Yet other Labour members remembered the divisions of 1979 and privately resolved on a cross-party coalition. And Blair had, the previous summer, readily accepted their views.

II

George Robertson had paid the price for the pre-election shambles over the referendum. Blair shifted him to Defence and turned instead to Donald Dewar, a shrewd chief whip in the last year of opposition but an expert on Scots politics from eleven years as shadow Secretary. He was charged with the drafting of the white paper, so his name was foregrounded in the first raft of senior ministers, alongside those of Chancellor and Foreign Secretary. This change altered the nature of the eventual 'yes-yes' campaign. Robertson, with the Scottish party's general secretary Jack McConnell, had begun planning it pre-election. They decided that the Constitutional Convention was not equipped to run a campaign nor would the SNP be likely to join such a campaign, given past opposition. They agreed with Kenyon Wright, the Convention's chairman, that an organisation was needed which was separate from the Convention but patently inspired by it. Nigel Smith, the managing director of David Auld Valves, a Glasgow manufacturing company, became chair of the new organisation – Scotland Forward. Too reserved for the media, he was highly intelligent, progressive and enthusiastic about home rule, giving him credibility with Labour and the Liberal Democrats. He was a businessman, so might attract individual pro-devolution Tories. His campaigns for Scottish autonomy in broadcasting also gave him credibility with the SNP.

Robertson had a visceral hatred of the SNP and saw Scotland Forward consisting of the Convention's partners plus individual Nationalists and Tories, with the SNP itself excluded. Dewar's view was that 'yes' unity required the SNP leadership on board Scotland Forward. The SNP were worried by election campaign statements by the pretty-well-unreconstructed Labour unionist Brian Wilson, now a Scottish Office minister, that only Westminster could make moves towards independence. Salmond and Mike Russell, the SNP's chief strategist, while they privately believed independence was more likely to come through an Edinburgh parliament, feared that any such statement in the white paper would make it impossible for the SNP to support a 'yes-yes' vote. Dewar told them that there would be no such statement, and although there would be many declarations that sovereignty, and therefore the power to make further constitutional changes, would remain at Westminster, in the practical political world, if an SNP majority in Edinburgh's parliament opted to hold an independence referendum, Westminster could not possibly prevent or ignore such a vote. After all, the Tory government had ditched water privatisation after a referendum run by Strathclyde Regional Council in 1993 resulted in its overwhelming rejection. The SNP's gradualist leaders were thus satisfied that they could safely join the 'yes-yes' campaign.

SNP policy had been for many years open to devolution and many voters had told canvassers during the election that devolution would be good for the party. Meeting in July, its national executive recommended to the national council (of constituency representatives) on 2 August in Perth that the party join. Two voices were raised against: Sillars, who argued from *The Sun* that devolution was a Labour snare, and Gordon Wilson, who had been deeply scarred by seeing the 1979 Assembly thwarted by Labour Party divisions after he worked all out for a 'yes' vote. Both were in a very small minority.

III

A 'no-no' campaign then emerged under the 'Think Twice' banner. It had a curious, and ultimately unhelpful, origin. Some Tories who gave up on the election long before polling day – such as Brian Monteith, a student 'no' activist in 1979, one of Forsyth's *fauves* in 1990 and now running his own public relations company in Edinburgh – started preparing to demand a referendum on devolution once Labour had won the election. These plans were halted when Labour announced its referendum but rapidly revived post-election. Donald Findlay, a Tory but with a higher profile as advocate, Rector of St Andrews and vice-chairman of Rangers (so much for collaring Catholic support . . .), was Monteith's key player, supposedly keeping 'Think Twice' at a distance from the party, which could back it without seeming to do so. At the party conference in Perth in June, where a high turnout of members voted overwhelmingly to campaign against Labour's plans (while accepting that some reprobates would campaign for a 'yes-yes' vote), involvement got more explicit. Monteith's hopes of a broad-based campaign withered; he could find no Labour politician nor any Scottish celebrity willing to join, nor much in the way of cash. Senior Tories remembered him as a Forsyth ally in the ruckus of 1988-90. So Monteith went. Lord Fraser of Carmyllie, an ex-minister, became director and Sir Matthew Goodwin, a former Tory Party treasurer, was brought in as treasurer. From then on money rolled in, to the tune of £150 000, but despite a press conference launch in Glasgow in August, with Findlay, Fraser and Goodwin, it was seen by all as a Tory front.

The organisation of the 'yes-yes' campaign was relatively simple. Scotland Forward was a neutral umbrella under which the three parties could gather for joint events; this helped neutralise objections in some Labour and SNP quarters about sharing platforms with the enemy. Its literature could be used by all parties and it helped coordinate their individual campaigns, with a common design for stickers, posters and leaflets which each party happily used in their own colours. Each party put out its own literature and did the limited canvassing that was possible, divided up on the rule of thumb that parties would lead in their own constituencies and council wards. With very few exceptions, such as in North Ayrshire where there were problems between Labour and SNP activists, local parties managed to bury their enmities by concentrating on their own patches and not coming into contact with each other.

From the outset the Labour Party led, not just because it held fifty-six of the seventy-two Scottish seats, but mainly because the government could not afford to fail. Labour's Scottish general secretary, Jack McConnell, used the

Figure 10.1 The Ridings.
Photograph by Marion Ralls.
The petitions for a Scottish Parliament are brought from all parts of Scotland to Parliament Square, Edinburgh, during the referendum campaign of 1997.

same organisational template that had won on 1 May. Dewar's junior minister, Henry McLeish, cleared his ministerial diary for four weeks and took charge of the campaign team in Keir Hardie House, as in the general election. Millbank also sent London-based staff such as Dave Hill, the well-regarded head of media relations, to Glasgow for the campaign. He had to prepare carefully, as polling among focus groups showed that the second question could be lost, though there were also ways of winning it. Women, for example, said that their fears of tax increases could be allayed if they thought the money raised would be spent on better schools or more jobs. Such data was fed back into the campaign – for example, via speeches and statements by Gordon Brown, the Chancellor.

Labour's overall strategy aimed to polarise the voters' choices around four themes: that the referendum meant Scotland versus the Tories; that the parliament was essential to Tony Blair's new Britain; that there would be no tax rises; and that it would mean Scots taking decisions on Scottish issues in Scotland. Without determined unity between the three parties, this strategy could have come badly unstuck. The SNP could have hyped up their belief that devolution would lead on to independence, and the Liberal Democrats could have stressed their election pledge to raise income tax in order to spend more on education. But both parties agreed to downplay these issues in order to get Labour's voters out on polling day, best done by putting Labour messages out.

In July, Dewar produced his white paper. Headed simply *Scotland's Parliament*, it was the biggest-selling document ever produced by the government in Scotland. It was pretty much the Convention scheme. It even gave a partial answer to the West Lothian question; Scotland's over-representation at Westminster would in due course be cut back from seventy-two to somewhere around fifty-eight. After presenting it in the Commons, ministers, Labour and opposition MPs, and journalists mixed cheerfully together on a chartered flight back to a reception at Edinburgh Castle. Dewar, in an unusual outburst of wild emotion, told the guests that the day had left him 'almost enthused'.

IV

He was not so excited, however, by start of the campaign. The Labour MP for Paisley South, Gordon McMaster, died on 30 July. Soon it emerged that he had committed suicide and had left a note blaming party colleagues, including the neighbouring MP for Renfrewshire West, Tommy Graham, for spreading smears about him. Media interest in the referendum abruptly switched to Paisley and as Labour's chief whip, Nick Brown, moved to investigate, allegations of factional in-fighting and political and financial corruption in Paisley preoccupied the media. It was still boiling away when 'yes-yes' was launched. A

Scotland Forward press conference on 19 August was supposed to focus on the heartening phenomenon of the leaders of three parties on the same platform, all saying the same thing. But the reporters wanted to know what Labour was going to do about Tommy Graham, by then fingered as the man at the centre of the Paisley scandal. Dewar was pressed again and again, but could only respond again and again that he could not anticipate Brown's inquiry. Salmond and Menzies Campbell (standing in for Jim Wallace) were forbearingly supportive, but the launch was a fiasco and the media got Labour on the rack. The Think Twice campaign produced posters featuring Graham and Mohammed Sarwar, the Glasgow Govan MP, who was also suspended for alleged election misconduct. Would these, they said, be the faces of a Scottish parliament?

But by late August, the 'yes-yes' campaign faced a more serious opponent. In a long interview with *The Scotsman*, Sir Bruce Patullo, governor of the Bank of Scotland, warned that the tax-raising power would be dangerous. His interview, given with the full backing of the bank's board, said that the bank was neutral about the principle of a Scottish parliament, but was concerned that higher levels of income tax in Scotland – which he put at £6 a week for a Scot on an average wage if the full 3p was levied – would damage business and jobs.

The SNP's research department produced figures contending that Sir Bruce was wrong but Labour sent in its biggest bruiser, John Prescott, the deputy Prime Minister, who did to the banker what he usually did to English syntax; Sir Bruce should stick to counting money as he did not know anything about politics. This demonstration convinced other business doubters to keep their mouths shut, while Dewar and McLeish assured business audiences that a parliament with tax-varying powers was safe. Scotland Forward also produced a dozen entrepreneurs, including Sir Lewis Robertson, a former chairman of the Scottish Development Agency, who backed a report from the Scottish Council Foundation, a satellite of the Scottish Council Development and Industry, which argued that business had nothing to fear from devolution.

Think Twice feebly countered this by parading a few farmers who feared a central Scotland-dominated parliament, but by the end of August, the business case against devolution was undermined, divided and effectively sidelined. Its campaign was further derailed by a silly speech by Michael Ancram, the Tory constitutional spokesman, in Aberdeen, likening the Tory stand against devolution to Churchill against Nazi Germany before World War II. Michael Heseltine had pulled something similar off in Edinburgh shortly before polling day in 1992, but this time the press tore Ancram (kinsman of Lord Lothian, a notorious appeaser . . .) apart.

Then, in the small hours of Sunday, 31 August, such controversy slammed to a halt. Diana Princess of Wales was killed in a car crash. Britain, especially south-east England, plunged into an almost unbelievable orgy of mourning.

All campaigning, except a limited amount of leafleting, stopped. Would some sense of Britishness evoked by the tragedy cause people to step back from courting 'the break-up of Britain'? But this was countered by a distinct sense of hostility to the royal family and recoil from the 'recreational grief' of London. One oddball reaction probably helped the 'yes-yes' campaign. Jim Farry, chief executive of the Scottish Football Association, decided not to reschedule the Scotland v Belarus World Cup qualifier in Aberdeen that day, despite media and public rage, and even when the players, spectators and the Belarusians themselves wanted the game moved.

Dave Hill realised that Farry, already loathed by the media, was now the most hated man in Scotland. He decided that Dewar should pitch in, winning credit whether Farry gave way or not, and phoned BBC Scotland and Scottish Television while their 6.30 p.m. news programmes on 2 September were on air;

Figure 10.2 Death of a Princess, 31 August 1997.
Photograph provided by *The Herald*.
The royal family holed up in Balmoral, though arguably the Scots were both respectful to them and less than possessed by the hysteria which gripped the London area over 'the people's princess'. Yet the flowers, and some pretty odd tributes, piled up in Glasgow's George Square.

Dewar was contacting the SFA to express his 'grave concern'. Dewar duly did so, followed next day by Blair. That evening, Farry caved in.

A week's suspension left only three effective days of campaigning. How to re-energise public interest? Blitz the media with celebrities. The SNP's top star Sean Connery, on the Sunday before polling day, took a boat trip across the Forth with Gordon Brown. Later he joined Dewar, Salmond and Wallace in a Scotland Forward event in New Parliament House, and spoke from the Declaration of Arbroath. However corny, the resulting pictures made every television bulletin and even *The Financial Times*. On Monday Blair visited schools and took questions from television viewers. Prescott was back on Tuesday. The 'yes-yes' campaign received an unexpected boost from Brian Souter, the Stagecoach millionaire, who declared that a parliament would 'galvanise and motivate our public life'. Business opinion was now serving devolution.

Figure 10.3 'Avoiding eye contact?'
Photograph provided by *The Scotsman*.
The Diana truce called off, Sean Connery comes back from Marbella to meet his old foe, the British Chancellor, and launch the hundred-hour campaign. Connery was generously subsidising the SNP, which seems to have led Donald Dewar to deny him a knighthood in the summer of 1998, one of a chapter of accidents which befell Labour at that time.

On TV and radio Dewar tamed 'no-no' campaigners. Up against Dalyell, his wit and intellectual agility made heroic Tam look a pedantic bore. An aide later admitted that if the opposition knew its stuff it could have given Dewar a tougher time, but after twenty years polishing the devolution case, it would have taken a Nobel prizewinner to have laid a glove on him. Think Twice had only one celeb, who brought the charisma of Herod visiting an orphanage. By accident rather than design, Lady Thatcher was in Glasgow on 9 September to address American travel agents. She dutifully inveighed against devolution. A 'no-no' man moaned to John Maxton MP, campaigning in Glasgow's Buchanan Street, that he wished she was on the other side: 'Then the Scots would vote 'no-no' to spite her!'

On polling day the newspapers were (almost) solid. 'Today we make history,' proclaimed *The Scotsman*'s headline. 'Dewar set for dual role,' said *The Herald*, assuming a vote for home rule and predicting that Dewar would lead the new administration in Edinburgh while continuing to be Scottish Secretary. *The Express* forecast 'A New Chapter' in Scottish history, abandoning its usual Tory stance. 'Vote For Us. Vote Yes! Yes!' shouted the *Daily Record* alongside a picture of happy multiracial tots. 'X Marks the Scot' chimed in *The Sun* (though it campaigned venomously against the Welsh Assembly). Only the *Daily Mail* muttered gloomily about: 'The £280m Bill for a Double Yes Vote.' That evening, Thursday, 11 September, Scotland's chattering classes – politicians who had fought for and against constitutional change, journalists who had chronicled it, academics who had analysed it, celebrities who had poked their heads out of one ivory tower or another – drifted into the Edinburgh International Conference Centre 'hatbox' to see the results.

The mood was sober, not just because all that was around to celebrate or drown sorrows was coffee and fizzy water, accompanied strangely by bagels and ciabatta. For most, the campaign was as remarkable as blue sky and green grass; 'yes-yes' was ahead on the first question, perhaps 70–30 at best, and on the second question, maybe 60–40 at the outside. Uneasy jokes circulated: North Lanarkshire voters had all spoiled their second ballot papers because they were green. But there was worry about turnout: only 55 per cent, only 50 per cent. Was this good enough?

The Tory 'no-no' folk tended to huddle in groups. They conceded the first question, but anxiously calculated on getting a 'no' on the tax-raising powers. Dewar, swept in, flanked by advisers and television lights, and stayed silent, adding to the slight air of worry. It was all over with the first result. A remarkable 66.1 per cent had turned out to vote in Clackmannanshire. Even more stunningly, 80 per cent voted 'yes' to question one and 69 per cent to the tax-raising powers. It was all over bar the recording of the results from the other thirty-one local authorities.

To a general air of disbelief, the legacy of 1979 and 1992, the Scots had broken the defeat-from-the-jaws-of-victory habits of a generation. The turnout was big, 60.4 per cent, which party organisers estimated was equivalent to a true turnout of 71 per cent given that the electoral register was eleven months out of date and some 15 per cent of the names on it could not vote because they had died or moved house. Of those who voted, 74.3 per cent voted for the parliament and 63.5 per cent for tax-varying powers. Only in two areas, Orkney and Dumfries and Galloway, was there a 'no' vote, and those were narrowly (52.6 per cent and 51.2 per cent respectively) against only the tax-varying power. As percentages of the Scottish electorate, 44.8 per cent voted 'yes' to the first question and 38.4 per cent voted 'yes' to the second. Applying the same adjustment to the electoral register as was applied in 1979 to discount the dead, even the second question would have passed that referendum's infamous rule that 40 per cent of the electorate had to consent to the proposal.

On 11 September, the Scots did not just agree to their parliament; they thumped the table and demanded it. The result was emphatically what John Smith had claimed – 'the settled will of the Scottish people' – and could not now, as the Tories were commendably quick to accept, be undone except by that same will.

The following week, the fate of the Welsh Assembly was decided. Rather oddly, although it was backed (more than the Scottish parliament had been) by both sides of industry, the Assembly came into being by a majority of less than 1 per cent. The timing was fortunate in view of subsequent revelations about the sources of Labour funding and the private life of Ron Davies, the Welsh Secretary of State. Nevertheless, the long-sought constitutional revolution, achieved by commendably constitutional means, was under way. The Scotland Act, the first clause of which splendidly stated 'There shall be a Scottish Parliament', began its progress through the two Houses of Parliament, which it would complete by mid-November 1998. Ominously few MPs participated in these rather dry debates; fewer still seemed interested in going to Holyrood.

This was a little odd, since the new parliament was certainly not going to be any 'toytown assembly'. The Scotland Act 1997 stood one aspect of the Scotland Act 1978 on its head. Whereas the 1978 Act listed everything that was to be devolved to the assembly, the 1997 Act listed everything which was to be kept under the control of Westminster. Since defining the 'reserved' powers was much easier than listing the 'devolved' powers, it made the negotiations with Whitehall easier and drafting the bill much simpler. The negotiations were tough. The Department of Trade and Industry, for example, was reluctant to cede control over industrial aid, fearing that a Scottish government could out-bid English regional development agencies with subsidies for inward-investing companies. The solution to this and similar problems, such as Scottish dealings with the European Commission, was to draft sets of rules, called 'concordats', which everybody would agree to abide by.

Crucial to this whole process was a group of senior Scottish Office civil servants who were formed into a Constitution Group – loosely before the 1997 election and more firmly during the election campaign – to do battle with Whitehall. Their work – for example, on how to separate out the management and regulation of the energy industries (reserved to Westminster) from control of the environmental aspects of these industries (devolved to Scotland) – was just as important as the political slogging – resisting pressure to take proportional representation out of the scheme, for example – that Dewar had to do on the devolution Cabinet committee to get the Convention scheme through. The Cabinet committee was gruelling. The chair of it, Lord Irvine, the Lord Chancellor, subjected all the plans to a searching judicial examination which at times exhausted Dewar.

What emerged was substantial. The parliament would have power over a budget which, by 2000, would be close to £15 billion. It would not only spend this money on, but be able to make laws about, a wide range of areas relating to daily Scottish life: health, nursery to university education, all the work of local government including social work and housing, some aspects of economic development such as support for business and tourism, the administration of European structural funds, many transport matters and especially spending on roads, the legal and prison system, environmental protection, agriculture and forestry, fisheries management, sport and the arts. The SNP complained about such things as the lack of power over broadcasting and the circumscribed rights of representation in the European Union, but on no point was the government assailed by popular protest.

By and large, the debate was deeply technical. Much time was spent discussing precisely who would have to pay the 3p income tax levy if the parliament used that power. For example, the Bill defined as someone liable to pay the tax a person who had his or her main home in Scotland or spent more days in Scotland than in the rest of Britain, a day in Scotland being defined as being north of the border at the end of that day. (People who live in Carlisle but work in Dumfries would, if they worked a day shift, escape the Scottish tax; but if they worked a night shift, they would be caught by it.) And so the debates dragged on and on, for about 200 hours. Important and valuable, but mind-numbingly tedious, not least for Henry McLeish, the minister steering it through. Some changes were made, not just in clarifying who would be liable to the tartan tax. After complaints about political interference, the power of parliament to appoint and dismiss judges was curbed, an important provision. The last debate,

Figure 10.4 Not Calton Hill after all: the new Royal Bank of Scotland pound note.
Permission to reproduce granted by The Royal Bank of Scotland.
Donald Dewar deserts the 1979 Assembly building and announces that the Parliament building will occupy the old Holyrood Brewery site opposite the Palace of Holyroodhouse, to be opened by 2003. After a rather hurriedly arranged competition, the Catalan architect Enric Miralles won, with a futuristic design originally (he said) devised out of leaves and grass, later refined into a pattern of 'upturned boats'. As elaborated, with offices for MSPs, it looked rather middle-aged, and very expensive.

appropriately enough, got stuck in the mudbanks of the Solway Firth when trying to define where the border lines of civil jurisdiction should be drawn. Burns would have given a grim smile.

V

The dull normality of politics was paralleled by a feeling of cultural exhaustion. The Glasgow Mayfest closed down in 1997; Scottish Ballet was threatened; Julian Spalding, Glasgow's cultural head, resigned in an atmosphere of increasing admission charges and closures. After a period when the arts had been the propellant of autonomy, they now seemed secularly challenged by politics, in a similar way to the churches. The Edinburgh Festival was too big and many of the acts on its rampant Fringe had few enough connections with Scottish or, for that matter, any culture. The great figures of Scottish poetry took their leave – Norman MacCaig, Sorley Maclean, George Mackay Brown, Iain Crichton Smith – and critics found it difficult to see any respectable succession in the commercialised obscenity of Irvine Welsh.

The Scottish economy was suddenly looking worryingly fragile again. In early 1998 the price of crude oil was down to $11 a barrel, and tough bargaining would be needed between the state and the companies if the North Sea fields were to survive. The price of semi-conductors tumbled into the cellar, from $42 to under $2, threatening to bring down many of the Silicon Glen industries lured in by Locate in Scotland. Changes in Common Agriculture Policy and the high pound sterling threatened the country's already declining family farms. On top of this, the East Asian slump cut the market for whisky and tweeds. Infrastructural connections with the South were poor and would take long to improve, after the near-disaster of rail privatisation.

Yet there were also new signs of optimism from unexpected quarters. The Tories' programme of privatisation in the 1980s, which it had been feared would simply produce easy pickings for corporate predators, turned out to have produced Scottish seekers of prey. Scottish capitalism appeared to be in rude health, with ScottishPower, the Stagecoach bus group and the Royal Bank of Scotland raiding world-wide from their northern headquarters. But for how long? The rapid concentration of European finance after the introduction of the Euro foreboded a City takeover of many independent Scots financial institutions. General Accident merged with Commercial Union. Even the cherished mutual-ownership basis for the independence of the big Scottish life assurance companies looked distinctly wobbly when Scottish Amicable botched its attempt to demutualise and was promptly gobbled up by the Prudential insurance company.

Politically, the cross-party *bonhomie* dissipated smartly after the referendum campaign. Labour and the SNP slugged out a bitter parliamentary by-election in Paisley South, though Labour held on. An equally polarised campaign ensued in the European constituency of North-east Scotland following the death of Allan Macartney, the SNP MEP. The loss of his elder statesman wisdom was a blow to the Nationalist cause, but the party's romping victory in the November 1998 by-election was a more than balancing fillip. Traumatic for Labour was the fact that it was pushed into third place by the Tories, who convinced themselves that their fortunes were reviving.

Opinion polls gave conflicting accounts of the Scottish political mood. Polls by System Three for *The Herald* consistently stated that Labour and the SNP were running neck and neck, while both the Tories and the Liberal Democrats were trailing badly. Polls by ICM for *The Scotsman* also consistently found that Labour had a lead over the SNP, sometimes large, sometimes small, but never comfortably so for Labour. The possibility that the SNP might come close to winning the Scottish parliament elections seemed very real. Opinions about independence appeared to support this possibility. Questions about support for independence versus devolution in late 1998 found that independence was apparently almost as attractive as devolution. But interestingly, when the

Figure 10.5 Provost Pat Lally, 'a man with more comebacks than Lazarus', fights on.
Photograph provided by *The Herald*.

Labour got itself into difficulties in west Central Scotland, with scandals affecting the party in
Paisley, Govan and Glasgow Corporation. But even after all this upheaval, the first-past-the-post
system enabled Labour to convert 49 per cent of the Glasgow Council vote, on 6 May 1999, to
over 90 per cent of the City's Council seats.

adjective 'separate' was added to independence, support in polls dropped off quite dramatically.

Such checks on the expectation of Scottish independence were important, for otherwise it seemed something had gone wrong. Why hadn't devolution killed the challenge of the SNP, as George Robertson said it would do? The spin-doctoring of Labour's élite seemed dysfunctional north of the border. 'Cool Britannia' – conceived supposedly by the Foreign Office as a balancing formula to devolution – didn't play at all. The Millennium Dome at Greenwich was seen as yet another financial injection into the privileged South-east, although candidates to be mayor of London found it useful to assault what they claimed were disproportionate subsidies to Scotland. In November 1998, just as the Scotland Act was nearing royal assent, a report from the House of Commons Scottish Select Committee under the chairmanship of David Marshall, a Labour MP, put devolution under hostile scrutiny. Had any effective checks been written into the process? Was the division of responsibilities between Holyrood and Westminster logical? What were the Westminster MPs and the Secretary of State actually going to do?

Labour's candidate selection process provided more grist to the Nationalist mill. The party had abandoned the old system whereby any member, provided they could get support from the trade union and local government cabals in each constituency, could get nominated. Fearful of getting a solid phalanx of trade unionists and elderly councillors, the party opted for a panel system. Aspirant members of the Scottish Parliament (MSPs) had to be interviewed by a panel which assessed their skills of communication, political ability and loyalty. Constituency parties could only choose from those who made it on to this list. Unsurprisingly, few candidates made it from the Central Belt fiefdoms – Paisley or Motherwell; they had few women activists and fewer meetings. Labourites from the likes of South Edinburgh and Glasgow Kelvingrove, once the redoubts of the Tories, predominated heavily over trade unionists. For a first attempt, the outcome was rather ominous.

Besides some home rule enthusiasts and local government power wielders – Bob McLean, Isobel Lindsay and Mark Lazarowicz – who vanished through the screening process, two Westminster MPs, Ian Davidson, Glasgow Govan, and Denis Canavan, Falkirk West, failed to make it. Canavan, a maverick left-winger and habitual back-bench rebel, was furious. Campaigning for a Scottish parliament had been a life-long commitment, he fumed, and he was damned if New Labour apparatchiks were going to stop him getting into it. New Labour, rather surprisingly, failed to point out that other left-wing rebels such as Malcolm Chisholm, MP for Edinburgh Leith, and John McAllion, MP for Dundee East, had made it through the vetting system. Canavan, it soon became plain, would have plenty of constituency support as an Independent candidate.

For the SNP, this was glorious evidence that the Scottish Labour Party was not really Scottish at all but run from London. Millbank was clearly in charge and Blair was pulling all the strings, they crowed. The media always love a rebel and gave Canavan acres of space. The terribly handsome Tommy Sheridan got only slightly less coverage for his Scottish Socialist Party, threatening Labour's Glasgow vote from the left. In truth, however, these were minor irritants to the Labour Party, for the main threat was clearly from the Nationalists.

Gordon Brown had been detailed by Blair to take charge of the Scottish campaign after the drubbing in the North-east Euro by-election. The chronicler of the hardships endured by Red Clydesider James Maxton decided, in the words of one of his aides who went north from the Treasury with him, to take a baseball bat to the SNP. He would whack them hard over the costs of independence, again and again. An opening party political broadcast, featuring shattering glass and bleak wastelands, grimly warned that 'divorce is an expensive business' (perhaps a third of the population could mutter amen to that) and set the negative tone of Labour's campaign.

This was undoubtedly Alex Salmond's severest test since becoming SNP leader. At general elections, with the focus on the battle between the Tories and Labour, the Nationalists are a bit of a sideshow, even in Scotland. This election, however, would put him and his party under the spotlight. The SNP had plenty of evidence to show that Scots had not voted for the parliament out of some sense of braveheart patriotism or in the belief that they would rush on to independence, but because they thought it would lead to better public services and therefore a better standard of living. That pretty much fitted with Salmond's long-term perspective that Scots would only vote for independence once they had seen that a devolved parliament works. So Salmond's plan was to put forward a programme to make devolution work, demoting independence to last of a ten-point programme and positioning the SNP slightly to the left of Labour, accusing it of being London-controlled and continuing to roll out Tory policies.

This was no problem to Salmond, who is both a master of economic detail and an astute strategist, but it worried some in his party, such as Margo MacDonald, candidate in Edinburgh South, who saw little point in the SNP unless it was charging headlong towards independence. Nevertheless, she and other doubters maintained party discipline, which was severely tested by a pre-election gauntlet thrown down by Brown. In his March budget, he announced that the basic rate of income tax would be cut by 1p to 22p from April 2000. This threw Salmond and his lieutenants into a frenzy of debate. Should they announce that they would use 1p of the parliament's tax-varying power which would raise, thanks to Brown's widening of the basic-rate income tax band, about £220 million a year for public services? It could be presented, after all, not as a tax increase but as a tax standstill, that Scots would forego the tax 'bribe' that Brown was presenting to middle England. But on the other hand, it would mean Scots paying more income tax than the English, and the SNP would be isolated as the only party promising to use the tax-varying power. Salmond's argument for using the tax power prevailed, and was enthusiastically endorsed by the party at a conference in Aberdeen. The SNP produced millions of 'penny for Scotland' leaflets, yet this mildly redistributionist policy (about 1.9 million voters, twice as many as have ever voted SNP at a single election, would not pay the tax) did not do the expected trick.

This was not because the Scots had suddenly turned into eager consumers of low-tax political orthodoxy. The Tories, without their high-profile leaders Rifkind and Forsyth, were led by David McLetchie, an Edinburgh lawyer who was unknown to the public. They made little impact despite some eye-catching gimmicks and some unexpectedly impressive TV performances by McLetchie. It was more because the SNP failed to specify where the money would be spent, beyond gesturing vaguely at housing, education and health. This did not fit with the purposeful competence Salmond usually exuded.

Labour also hammered on about the financial plight an independent Scotland would find itself in. There is plenty of evidence that more public money is spent in Scotland than is raised in taxes, leaving a financial shortfall which ranges, in conventional economic terms, from being just about manageable to necessitating either tax increases or public spending cuts. Just how bad this deficit is depends a lot on North Sea oil tax revenues and that in turn depends on the price of oil. By the election, this was down to $10 a barrel, barely enough to justify sucking it out of the ground. Worse still for the SNP, a study commissioned by *The Economist* in January had found that an independent Scotland would not get a flat 90 per cent share of oil revenues as had usually been assumed, but a share which, because of cost write-offs against tax, falls as the oil price falls. At the election, the Scottish share of revenues was down to about 66 per cent. This posed a difficult question which the SNP spent much of the election evading with the aid of some slightly helpful comments from a couple of academic economists. Eventually Salmond, after denying that there was a financial shortfall, was forced into conceding that there was one, albeit smaller than everyone else claimed but still a deficit. Rather more successfully, the SNP tried to hit back at Labour's use of private finance to build public projects, claiming that this would cost taxpayers a fortune and was, in effect, privatising schools and hospitals built in this way. This caused Labour a lot of discomfort, but some behind-the-scenes arm-twisting of trade union leaders by Brown kept mutiny in bounds.

Frustratingly for the SNP leadership, the campaign refused to get into top gear because TV and the papers were full of the war in the Balkans. Early in the election campaign, Salmond had to make a broadcast reply to the Prime Minister's statement. He condemned the war as being of 'dubious legality' and the bombing of Serbia as an act of 'unpardonable folly', a statement that he insisted he made out of principle. Labour sent in its own heavy bombers – Robin Cook, Foreign Secretary, and George Robertson, Defence Secretary – and dropped 'the toast of Belgrade' label on Salmond. Canvassers reported that Salmond's statement provoked anger amongst voters, troublesome for the

Figure 10.6
Sean Connery.
Portrait by John Bellany. Provided by the Scottish National Portrait Gallery. Connery hated the Bond image, but his early fame still saw him supporting Scottish cultural projects. Bellany's fine portrait captures 'the smiler with the knife', who performed as brilliantly in Shakespeare as in Hitchcock.

SNP as their campaign was heavily, almost exclusively, dependent on him. While the polling evidence indicates that it did not seriously damage the SNP's chances, it increased the media's aggressiveness towards the party.

The one thing the SNP had not bargained on was the media being this hostile. They were used to tough questioning, but Salmond usually relied on his wit to defuse a problem. This time it didn't work. The tough questions kept on coming, on tax, on spending, on the cost of independence. Indeed the press, with the exception of *The Herald* which was editorially neutral but whose news coverage had a sympathetic lean towards the SNP, maintained a pretty solid anti-Nationalist front. The Labour-supporting *Daily Record* particularly enraged the Nationalists on the eve of a morale-boosting visit by Sean Connery. A front-page headline next to a days-old picture of the actor lashing out at American photographers blared: 'You've seen the polls then, Sean.' The SNP did not object when the same newspaper doled out worse to the Tories, but they certainly objected now. *The Scotsman*, *The Express*, *The Sun*, the *Daily Record*, the *Mirror* all declared for new Labour. The *Daily Mail* told people to vote for anybody but the SNP.

VI

And on polling day, 6 May 1999, which all the morning's headlines declared was a historic day for all Scots, only 59 per cent of voters could struggle along to the polling booth to make history. (71 per cent voted in the 1997 general election.) It may be that the rather negative nature of the campaign did not inspire a bigger turnout. It was also a complicated vote in the polling station. People had one paper to mark in the usual way for a constituency MSP. Then there was a foot-long paper to mark for the additional party list MSPs. And finally there was a third ballot paper, for the local council elections being held on the same day. Counting proved a long and weary process.

None of the major parties had given much thought about how to prevent people from changing their vote (or indeed how to encourage people to change) between the first and second ballots. In strong Labour areas where in truth there was not much point in people voting Labour again on the second paper, the others did make some effort to persuade people to switch to them. This may have hit Labour because it took 39 per cent of the first vote and only 34 per cent of the second vote, yielding it fifty-six seats, nine short of an overall majority. But neither the Tories, the SNP nor the Liberal Democrats picked up many of the Labour defectors. The SNP, as expected, came in second with 29 per cent and 27 per cent (thirty-five seats), the Tories third with 16 per cent and 15 per cent (eighteen seats), and the Liberal Democrats fourth with 14 per cent and 12 per cent (seventeen seats). The defectors, it seemed, preferred the small

Figure 10.7 A photocall for the first Scottish Cabinet, 10 May 1999.
Photograph provided by *The Scotsman*.
Dewar had to go into coalition with the Liberal Democrats, who furnished two out of an eleven-strong cabinet.
From left to right behind Dewar: Wendy Alexander, Communities; Lord Hardie, Lord Advocate; Jack McConnell, Finance; Tom McCabe, Parliament; Jim Wallace (LibDem), Justice, Home Affairs and Deputy First Minister; Henry McLeish, Enterprise and Lifelong Learning; Sam Galbraith, Children and Education; Susan Deacon, Health; Ross Finnie (LibDem), Rural Affairs; and Sarah Boyack, Transport and Environment. Boyack is also the daughter of the late Jim Boyack, a home rule stalwart since the days of the Covenant.

parties, whose share of the vote rose from 3 per cent to 11 per cent on the second ballot. The Greens gained an MSP in the Lothians (and Britain its first green parliamentarian) in Robin Harper. Tommy Sheridan, figurehead of the Scottish Socialist Party, got home in the Glasgow regional seat. And in Falkirk West, Dennis Canavan romped home, to the private delight of many old Labourites. Attempts to achieve gender balance yielded 37 per cent of women MSPs, a proportion exceeded only by Sweden and a big improvement on 1992, when Scotland sent only five women to Westminster. But – although the parliament was welcomed by 'New Scots', the Chief Rabbi noting that the Scots, almost uniquely in Europe, had never persecuted his people – ethnic minorities fared ill, in Wales as well as Scotland, and went without representation.

Home rule had arrived and the Scottish parliament had been elected, the first, indeed to be democratically elected. It was clearly going to have its own awkward squad. On 12 May 1999, 292 years after the last Scottish parliament voted itself out of existence a few hundred yards away in Parliament Hall behind St Giles' Church, 113 years after the Scottish Home Rule Association was set up, 111 years after Keir Hardie declared home rule to be part of the founding platform of the Labour Party, sixty-five years after the founding of the Scottish National Party, ten years after the Scottish Constitutional Convention was formed, and five years to the day since the death of John Smith, the Scottish parliament was duly reconstituted.

And at 11.52 a.m. in the venerable Assembly Hall of the Church of Scotland, originally the property of the Free Churchmen who had in 1842 signed the Claim of Right and had organised the Disruption a year later, and where the Scottish Constitutional Convention held its first meeting, Winnie Ewing, the woman whose by-election victory thirty-two years previously had sparked the modern drive towards home rule and who was now the oldest member of the new parliament, could say: 'The Scottish parliament, adjourned on the 25th day of March 1707, is hereby reconvened.'

Epilude

And after, in the Bow Bar,
we toast our halfway house
with Independence Whisky,
our parliament of rookies,
a score of well-kent faces
among a hundred unknowns,
a thousand-fingered beast
at Scotland's greasy till,
a parcel of rogues we know;
a shower of bastards, no doubt,
but at least, this time, at last,
they're our bastards.

Mike Dillon, 'New Parliament',
Poetry Scotland, no. 9

I

'A journey that has no end' was Donald Dewar's concluding line on the opening day, 1 July 1999, of the Scottish Parliament – for unionists perhaps too close to Parnell's 'No man can set a boundary to the march of a nation.' Even those who shared Dewar's federalistic unionism had doubts about the future. The Parliament wasn't just an addition to the economic and social tendencies within the country, but a self-willed instrument. If Scotland had been, since the Union, in the role of a voyager on Scott's placid but swift river, she was now being handed a paddle, just as the rapids were looming up. But how big a paddle? In the election campaign before 6 May much was made by Labour of the threat of 'separation' or 'divorce' posed by the SNP, yet the 'positive' mechanics of Anglo-Scottish relations had not figured as a theme. Was there anything to be positive about? Or had Labour dodged the issue by handing its campaign to Westminster Chancellor Gordon Brown, not First Minister Dewar or Prime Minister Blair?

In fact, the simplest explanation is that politicians tend to worry about winning elections first and then work out philosophies later to suit the results they get. Indeed, it seems that only Gordon Brown was giving much thought to cross-border relations. On the eve of the millennium, he gave a densely argued speech to a slightly baffled Scottish Labour audience in Edinburgh. Scottish politics, he contended, is not about national identity but the realisation of values of fairness and social justice. When these values were denied, whether in the time of Keir Hardie or John Smith, demand for home rule was one way of expressing them. Now that home rule had been achieved, the key task was to realise those values which, he said, meant Edinburgh and London working together and leaving the SNP in the cul-de-sac of identity politics. So he announced the creation of joint Westminster-Edinburgh-Cardiff-Belfast ministerial committees which would collaborate in dealing with child and pensioner poverty, and take action to meet the economic challenge of the information technology revolution.

The SNP insisted that what was happening here was the shackling of Holyrood to Westminster's agenda. In practice, common sense says that where there is a common political agenda, it is better for politicians to work together rather than separately. But was there, in the quadrilateral arrangement, an unsuspected potential for a federal Britain to emerge? Especially when one considers that one of the strange products of the Northern Irish political deal was a British-Irish Council, more romantically known as the Council of the Isles? Actually a sop to Ulster Unionists, it nevertheless created a new beast in the British constitution – a forum where the governments of Britain and Ireland, the devolved executives of Ulster, Scotland and Wales, and the forgotten governments of the Isle of Man, Jersey and Guernsey can, indeed must, meet and thrash out common problems.

But before this nascent federalism could become more fully-fledged, the uncertainties of Ulster plus the postponement of the comprehensive reform of English regional government meant that mechanisms were necessary to couple up the Westminster and Holyrood legislatures. For a start, Whitehall departments and the Scottish Office prepared 'concordats' delimiting their powers and those of their Holyrood counterpart: agreements between two executive arms of government, not constitutional treaties between the parliaments. They are non-statutory, which means that any subsequent executives, or indeed the current executives, could tear them up. The problem was their relation to ministerial responsibility.

For example, one concordat set rules so that the Scots could not use their devolved power over industrial subsidy to outbid other offers of aid by English regions or indeed Wales to foreign companies wanting to set up factories in Britain. In Labour's eyes, that was merely a sensible protection of taxpayers' money. But the SNP thought it a gross infringement of Scottish autonomy. And was Scotland's industry minister responsible here to the Scottish parliament or accountable, via the concordat, to the Treasury?

II

By an unwritten convention of pre-devolution times, Scottish MPs had been barred from holding Whitehall portfolios which were handled in Scotland by Scottish ministers. John Major dispensed with this when he moved Michael Forsyth to the Home Office, and Tony Blair's rather presidential style which, like that of Lady Thatcher, preferred working groups to cabinets, allowed plenty of Scots to continue at all levels of government.

But if this dynamic centralism faltered, what would happen to the 'territorial ministers', or UK ministers sharing portfolios with devolved counterparts? Not least the prehensile post of Scottish Secretary of State? Far from abolishing it, or amalgamating it into a Constitutional Affairs ministry covering the territories of Scotland, Wales and Northern Ireland, Blair appointed to it the 'big hitter', Dr John Reid, although with a budget of only £5 million or so Reid had little to hit with. In fact, this little conundrum was but part of the puzzle posed by the unfinished nature of Blair's constitutional reforms. What would Britain come to look like? Would it have a federal or semi-federal constitution, perhaps with an elected second chamber at Westminster with the nations and regions represented in it? Would it be part of a European political, economic and monetary union, or not? It was dreadfully unclear. What was clear, however, was that as each piecemeal change was made, the Scots would constantly have to reassess their position in the British and the European Unions.

III

The lesson of the previous 292 years offers two contradictory thoughts here. The first is that political parties which straddled the border strengthened the union. The most important role in this remit had fallen to Labour, and yet it was singularly ill-equipped to fulfil it. Its Scottish arm had spent much of the last quarter-century talking the language of nationalism, but after devolution, if it was true to what it said, it had to suddenly start talking the language of unionism. Brown's election role suggested another convention: the Whitehall Scot as regional boss. Someone like this was his finance minister equivalent in Helmut Kohl's Germany, Theo Waigel (he of the coypu eyebrows). The Bavarian Free State, though the birthplace of the federal constitution, exercised through its own conservative party, the Christian Social Union, a powerful role in the centre-right Christian Democrat administration, making up a quarter of the Bonn Cabinet. The vanishing of Scots Conservatism reinforced the argument for a British Labour version of this, but how many politicians of Brown's stature were there? And how solid was the Labour support that they could deliver?

Appreciation of the importance of the party as the cement in the Union edifice explained why Blair was so keen to maintain a tight control of the Labour Party's structures north of the border. But would it be wise to rein in autonomy of policy action? For the second lesson was that political parties thrived best in Scotland when they posed as the defenders and promoters of Scottish interests, especially when those interests conflicted with the will of other areas of the British Isles, which in practical political terms meant Westminster.

These conflicting political dynamics were at the root of the 'turf wars' between Reid and Dewar which broke out in the first months of the life of the Scottish Executive (as the devolved government is called) and the Scotland Office (as the non-devolved bit of Scottish government is called). Dewar had to be seen to be fighting for Scottish interests and knocking lumps out of Reid was apparently the easiest way of doing so. Yet these fisticuffs were staggeringly at odds with the language of partnership between Edinburgh and London with which Dewar launched Labour's election campaign. And if having a square go with Westminster and its satraps became perceived to be the model for Scottish political activity, the Nationalists were the obvious contenders to step into the ring if devolutionist first ministers got knocked out.

IV

On 6 May 1999 the SNP defeat showed the door to Holyrood's tax-varying powers, but the principle came back through the window as the Liberal Democrats' 'non-negotiable' commitment to free university education. What would happen to a UK higher education policy if tuition was free in Scotland and expensive elsewhere? While this was still under debate, Holyrood, following the Welsh Assembly, intervened in September 1999 with an attempt to bale out the country's hard-pressed livestock farmers. These schemes were ruled out of order by the European Commission, narrowly averting conflict with England's farming ministry. But the latent potential for dispute arose again when the devolved bodies maintained the ban on selling beef on the bone. Westminster, despite advice from the chief medical officer for health in England that the ban could be lifted, moved to the 'devolved' position, but with great misgivings. Its argument seemed to be that any Scottish exceptionality had to be stopped, if need be by surrendering to it and thus making it British. But if the only way of London keeping key reserved subjects like social security and the media under control meant constant detailed concessions to the Scots or the Welsh, policy would be settled by horse-trading between central government and the devolved executives, not by Westminster MPs.

The initial, slightly uneasy, answer to these dilemmas was that they did not arise because power, both at Holyrood and Westminster, was in the hands of government ministers – the executives – not the parliaments. And, of course, it was highly convenient that the two executives were of the same basic political hue: Labour in London and (with LibDem edges) Edinburgh. Even the injection of LibDemmery into the system did not necessarily grate with London. Jim Wallace, the Scottish justice minister, was pleasantly surprised when Jack Straw, a rather right-wing Home Secretary given to berating 'Hampstead liberals', did not object to Wallace's freedom of information bill which was rather freer than Straw was proposing south of the border.

This stability-through-cooperation ought at least to ensure that the parliament could enjoy an initial few years untroubled by much political tension with London. And yet it was uneasy because MPs and MSPs untrammelled by ministerial office were quick to complain when the executive they were responsible for holding to account appeared to be kowtowing too much to the other executive. MSPs, including Labour ones, agitated for more generous treatment of asylum-seekers than the Home Office was prepared to grant and which the Scottish Executive had to administer. MPs, including some Labour ones, were perturbed that Blair's government would not lift the beef-on-the-bone ban in England. And, of course, Labour could not expect to be in power north and south of the border for ever. Once same-party chumminess went out of the window, trouble would be bound to come in the door. This could mean inter-parliament relations degenerating into Westminster assaults on the number of Scots MPs, and Treasury raids on the devolved budget, while Holyrood continually sought to ratchet up its devolved powers. That was where the absence of the kind of written-down constitutional rulebook, complete with a refereeing constitutional court, which governs federal–Länder relations in Germany could be costly.

A fascinating example of the potential for power to sway between Edinburgh and London arose with one of the hot topics of the first election campaign. Labour proposed that it might introduce motorway tolls, which of course the opposition parties opposed vigorously. Sarah Boyack, the environment and transport minister (also the daughter of the late Jim Boyack, founder of the Campaign for a Scottish Assembly), took fright and shelved the tolls scheme. Labour had enough road tax headaches already with complaints from rural areas and lorry companies about high fuel duties. But David Begg, a transport advisor to John Prescott, the deputy Prime Minister, came up with a neat solution to both problems shortly after the election: introduce and raise motorway tolls while reducing fuel duties. It appealed because it gave a (duty) quid pro (toll) quo. But the problem was that fuel taxes were Westminster's responsibility and motorway tolls were Edinburgh's function. If this policy solution ever became a real idea, how would it be resolved? By devolving Scottish fuel duties to Scotland, or by Westminster re-acquiring power over road tolls?

V

Another potential north–south link was the media, broadsheet small-n nationalism always being overshadowed by a tabloid attachment to soaps, soccer and sex which was authentically if (to fastidious politicians) dismayingly British. The British press is, in comparison with that of Germany – where *Bild* only reaches 19 per cent and most papers are solid *Scotsman*-type regionals – unspeakably primitive. The BBC was reluctant to concede any real degree of autonomy to Glasgow, and Anglo-global newspaper proprietors, though prepared to sup with devolution, set their faces against the SNP. Might there be a putative convention here, with press and broadcasting controlled by 'shuttle people' who bridged the ruling élites of Scotland and London?

This might be true of the leader columns but not of the 'devolved' news pages, all of which gave prominence to the SNP as the main opposition to Labour. Some power-brokers with high profiles – the dynamic Kirsty Wark and her husband and business ally Alan Clements – had an almost ambassadorial role, and others fancied one, notably Scotland's frantically ambitious Cardinal, Thomas Winning. And might fair-minded, in-house coverage be overshadowed by proprietorial ambitions to cuddle up to the government, exemplified by the battering that the press – headed by the unregenerate unionists Martin Clarke of the *Record* and Andrew Neil of *The Scotsman* – meted out to Salmond in the general election?

Again the last 292 years give a lesson. The media is but one of an array of Scottish civic establishments, and it is only when these establishments conclude that the union is not working to their liking that the constitutional foundations move. Agitation by municipal authorities and urban élites led to the institution of the post of Scottish Secretary in 1885. The fear of deindustrialisation and depopulation led industrialists to support Johnston's drive to extend the powers of the Scottish Office between 1941 and 1945. In the 1979 devolution referendum, opposition to devolution by prominent churchmen, the universities and big employers played a part in the defeat of the assembly proposals. But in the following two decades, experience of Thatcherism led the churches and universities to join with the local authorities and trade unions in supporting devolution while the business anti-devolution voice dwindled to a point at which it could barely be heard in 1997. And none of these civic institutions was at all disposed to see any advantage in independence.

The media, however, could affect things in other ways. It rapidly became obvious, once the parliament was elected, that the reptiles had declared open season on all MSPs, not just the SNP. Might this penalise Labour, which had more of them, or MSPs of all affiliations? Or would it damage the Nationalist cause, on the grounds that people would be reluctant to give such a shower even more power? Or would the victim turn out to be the Scottish-based media itself, ironically, as its support for devolution in the Thatcher era had been based on the calculation that a parliament would be good for sales? Its personnel certainly didn't mirror the 'feminised' parliament, and its agenda did not seem to match the public mood of warmth towards the new legislature.

VI

In the summer of 1999 the SNP was bogged down in its own election post-mortem, with Salmond under attack from an alliance between his party's right and its 'independence-first' wing. A vocal minority, including the treasurer, Ian Blackford, and Salmond's predecessor, Gordon Wilson, suspected that he wanted to sell out their independence birthright for a mess of devolution pottage and ministerial limousines. When George Robertson became NATO Secretary-General and went to the Lords, his Hamilton South seat at Westminster seemed safe. Yet such was now the Janus face of Scottish politics that the SNP ended only 556 votes behind the Labour man. The polls showed that New Labour at Westminster was well ahead of the SNP as far as a Westminster general election was concerned but only a nose in front of the SNP in Holyrood elections, and it was more on Holyrood than Westminster issues that Hamilton voted.

Bravura by-elections apart, the arrival of a devolved Scottish parliament presented a series of dilemmas to Nationalism as it is embodied in the SNP. Should it accept that devolution is the 'settled will' of the Scottish people or should it continue to press for independence? If the latter, is the route to this grail mapped out through Holyrood or Westminster?

In the opening months of the new devolved era, the SNP seemed to be saying it would do all of these things; it would try to make devolution work, it would still seek independence, it would try to get it in both Westminster and Holyrood elections. And despite the rhetoric disavowing Westminster and all its works, it was the SNP, with tactics which harassed the Executive at every turn, which seemed determined to import the allegedly despised Westminster politics into the supposedly more consensual Holyrood arena. The initial frantic and, at times, knee-jerk Nationalist oppositional activity may have been as much aimed at dissipating internal tensions as at exacerbating Labour-LibDem problems, for there remains the problem of defining independence and working out how to get it. Some Nationalists were privately satisfied with what Holyrood has got, some would add control of social security and broadcasting, some would want that plus foreign affairs and defence, some would want to be in NATO and some would not, most want to be in the EU but some do not; the independence spectrum is long and infinitely variable. Disputes about where to sit on this spectrum have caused there to be, at times, no less than four competing Nationalist parties in the Basque Country of Spain. There have been only slightly fewer fissiparous tendencies in Catalonia and Quebec. Could Alex Salmond prevent them erupting in his party?

Nevertheless, and probably later rather than sooner, the SNP would have to confront the catch-22 which dogs every Nationalist party in the developed democratic world. To win independence, you must first win power. But winning power usually means disavowing independence, as Jordi Pujol's Catalan Nationalist party and the PNV (Partido Nacionalista Vasco), the main Basque Nationalist party, have done to enjoy long periods of provincial power in Spain. To break through the glass ceiling of a third of the vote, which is the most the SNP has ever been able to achieve, should Salmond learn a lesson from Wales? Plaid Cymru eschewed independence as an immediate goal before the first Welsh Assembly elections and went on, quite unexpectedly, to deprive Labour of an expected majority in the Assembly, winning heartland South Wales Labour seats such as the Rhondda and Islwyn. If these were Alex Salmond's private strategic thoughts, and many in his party suspected so, they were kept private by the Hamilton result, which, Salmond asserted at his party conference, had produced a swing of 22 per cent, enough to give the SNP sixty-four out of the seventy-two Westminster seats.

May, 2000, as this book finally went to press, saw the completion of the Parliament's first year. Through its European-style committee system, a striking amount of legislation on which Westminster would have choked, such as feudal law abolition, was passed. The press, however, particularly the unwontedly political tabloids, was not kind. It allied with Brian 'Stagecoach' Souter's overmighty capital to attack Parliament's move to repeal Section 28, luridly screaming that homosexuality was being legitimated. Labour suffered at the first Scottish Parliament by-election, at Ayr on 16 March, coming in third. But the Tories, not the SNP, won. Fundamentalism didn't save Souter's share price, as investment surged to the dot.coms, but it was hard to see where the economic tide was heading. Oil income reached levels unseen since the early 1980s, but the high pound hammered factory after factory. The Royal Bank carried off National Westminster, but a Monaco-based carpetbagger set out to demutualise Standard Life, the jewel of Edinburgh's financial sector. Miralles's upturned boats at Holyrood seemed, cash-wise, to resemble upturned TITANICS, and people blamed Donald Dewar. But when the First Minister fell ill in May and underwent a heart operation, the concern and goodwill on all sides was patent. 'O brave new world, that hath such creatures in it.' The creatures were odd, true, but the new Scotland seemed brave enough to get by.

Acknowledgements

Sources are indicated beside each illustration. The publisher would like to thank the following for providing illustrations and granting permission for their reproduction in this edition. Every effort has been made to trace copyright holders, but if any have been inadvertently overlooked, the publisher will be pleased to make the necessary acknowledgement at the first opportunity.

T. and R. Annan & Sons Ltd, Glasgow
Avigdor Arikha
John Bellany
Lady Dunnett
Free Church of Scotland
Gordon Wright Photo Library
Alasdair Gray
The Herald
Alan Lawson
Mrs C. MacWhirter
Alexander Moffat
The Trustees of the National Library of Scotland
People's Palace, Glasgow
Punch
Radical Scotland
Marion Ralls
Felix Rosenstiel's Widow & Son Ltd
Royal Bank of Scotland
The Scotsman
Scottish National Party
Scottish National Portrait Gallery
School of Scottish Studies, University of Edinburgh
Scottish Theatre Archive

Bibliography

Aitken, Keith, *The Bairns o' Adam* (Edinburgh: Polygon, 1996)

Anderson, Robert, *Education and Opportunity in Victorian Scotland: Schools and Universities* (Oxford: Clarendon, 1983)

Ascherson, Neal, *Games with Shadows* (London: Verso, 1988)

Bowie, J. A., *The Future of Scotland* (Edinburgh: Chambers, 1939)

Brand, Jack, *The National Movement in Scotland* (London: Routledge, 1978)

Brown, Alice, David McCrone and Lindsay Paterson, *Politics and Society in Scotland* (London: Macmillan, 1998)

Brown, Gordon, ed., *The Red Paper on Scotland* (Edinburgh: Edinburgh Student Publications Board, 1975)

Cage, R. A., ed., *The Scots Abroad: Labour, Capital, Enterprise, 1750–1914* (London: Croom Helm, 1985)

Campbell, Roy, *The Rise and Fall of Scottish Industry* (Edinburgh: John Donald, 1980)

Cargill, Ken, ed., *Scotland 2000* (Glasgow: BBC, 1987)

Clements, Alan, Kenny Farquharson and Kirsty Wark, *Restless Nation* (Edinburgh: Mainstream, 1996)

Craig, David, *Scottish Literature and the Scottish People* (London: Chatto and Windus, 1961)

CREST, *Scotland and Wales: Nations Again* (Cardiff: University of Wales Press, 1999)

Cullen, L. M. and T. C. Smout, eds, *Comparative Aspects of Scottish and Irish Economic and Social History, 1600–1900* (Edinburgh: John Donald, 1974)

Cunnison, J. and J. B. S. Gilfillan, eds, *The Third Statistical Account of Scotland: Glasgow* (Glasgow: Collins, 1958)

Dalyell, Tam, *Devolution: The End of Britain* (London: Faber, 1977)

Davie, George Elder, *The Democratic Intellect: Scotland and her Universities in the Nineteenth Century* (Edinburgh: Edinburgh University Press, 1961)

Devine, Tom, *The Scottish Nation, 1707–1999* (London: Penguin, 1999)

Devine, Tom and Richard Findlay, eds, *Scotland in the Twentieth Century* (Edinburgh: Edinburgh University Press, 1996)

Donaldson, William, *Popular Literature in Victorian Scotland: Language, Fiction and the Press* (Aberdeen: Aberdeen University Press, 1986)

Donnachie, Iain et al., *Forward! – 100 Years of Labour Politics in Scotland* (Edinburgh: Polygon, 1988)

Drummond, A. L. and J. Bulloch, *The Church in Victorian Scotland, 1843–1874* (Edinburgh: St Andrew Press, 1975)

Edwards, Owen Dudley, ed., *A Claim of Right for Scotland* (Edinburgh: Polygon, 1988)

Ferguson, William, 'The Reform Act (Scotland) of 1832: Intention and Effect' in *The*

Scottish Historical Review, vol. 45 (1966)

Finlay, Richard, *Independent and Free* (Edinburgh: John Donald, 1994)

Fraser, W. Hamish, *Conflict and Class: Scottish Workers, 1700–1838* (Edinburgh: John Donald, 1988)

Fry, Michael, *Patronage and Principle: A Political History of Modern Scotland* (Aberdeen: Aberdeen University Press, 1987)

Gallagher, Tom, ed., *Nationalism in the Nineties* (Edinburgh: Edinburgh University Press, 1991)

Gibson, John S., *The Thistle and the Crown* (Edinburgh: Stationery Office, 1985)

Gray, Alasdair, *Why Scots should rule Scotland* (Edinburgh: Canongate, 1997)

Hanham, H. J., *Scottish Nationalism* (London: Faber, 1969)

——, 'The Creation of the Scottish Office, 1881–7' in *The Juridical Review*, vol. 10 NS (1965), pp. 205–36.

Harvie, Christopher, *Fool's Gold* (London: Penguin, 1994)

——, *No Gods and Precious Few Heroes: Scotland since 1914* (London: Arnold, 1981; revised edition, Edinburgh: Edinburgh University Press, 2000)

——, *Scotland and Nationalism* (London: Allen and Unwin, 1977; revised edition, London: Routledge, 1997)

——, *Travelling Scot* (Colintraive: Argyll, 1999)

Hassan, Gerry, *A Guide to the Scottish Parliament* (Edinburgh: Centre for Scottish Public Policy/Big Issue, 1999)

Hassan, Gerry and Chris Warhurst, eds, *A Different Future* (Edinburgh: Centre for Scottish Public Policy, 1999)

Hechter, Michael, *Internal Colonialism: The Celtic Fringe in British National Development* (London: Routledge, 1975)

Hunter, James, 'The Politics of Highland Land Reform, 1873–1895' in *Scottish Historical Review*, no. 53 (1974), pp. 46–63

Hutchison, Ian, *A Political History of Scotland, 1832–1922* (Edinburgh: John Donald, 1985)

Johnston, Thomas, *History of the Working Classes in Scotland* (Glasgow: Forward, 1921)

Keating, Michael and David Bleiman, *Labour and Scottish Nationalism* (London: Macmillan, 1979)

Kellas, J. G., *The Scottish Political System* (Cambridge: Cambridge University Press, 1973, 1989)

——, *Modern Scotland* (London: Pall Mall, 1968, 1980)

Knox, William, *Industrial Nation* (Edinburgh: Edinburgh University Press, 1999)

——, *Scottish Labour Leaders, 1920–1950* (Edinburgh: Mainstream, 1983)

Levitt, Ian, *Poverty and Welfare in Scotland, 1890–1948* (Edinburgh: Edinburgh University Press, 1988)

Linklater, Magnus and Robin Denniston, eds, *Anatomy of Scotland Today* (London: Chambers, 1992)

Lythe, S. G. E. and John Butt, *An Economic History of Scotland* (Glasgow: Blackie, 1975)

Macartney, Allan and David Denver, eds, *Yes or No: The Devolution Referendum* (Aberdeen: Aberdeen University Press, 1981)

McCrone, David, *Understanding Scotland* (London: Routledge, 1992)

MacDonald, Catriona, ed., *Unionist Scotland, 1800–1997* (Edinburgh: John Donald, 1998)

McLean, Ian, *The Legend of Red Clydeside* (Edinburgh: John Donald, 1982, 1999)

Marr, Andrew, *The Battle for Scotland* (London: Penguin, 1992)

Meikle, H. W., *Scotland and the French Revolution* (Glasgow: Maclehose, 1912)

Miller, Hugh, *My Schools and Schoolmasters* (Edinburgh: Edmonstone and Douglas, 1854)

Miller, W. L., *The End of British Politics: Scots and English Political Behaviour in the Seventies* (Oxford: Oxford University Press, 1981)

Mitchell, James, *Strategies for Self-government* (Edinburgh: Edinburgh University Press, 1996)

'Muir, James Hamilton' (James and Muirhead Bone), *Glasgow in 1901* (Glasgow: Maclehose, 1901)

Nairn, Tom, *Auld Enemies* (Glasgow: Common Cause, 1996)

——, *The Breakup of Britain* (London: Verso, 1977)

——, *The Enchanted Glass* (London: Verso, 1988)

——, *Faces of Nationalism* (London: Verso, 1997)

Paterson, Lindsay, *The Autonomy of Modern Scotland* (Edinburgh: Edinburgh University Press, 1994)

——, *A Diverse Assembly: The Debate on the Scottish Parliament* (Edinburgh: Edinburgh University Press, 1998)

Peat, Jeremy and Bill Jamieson, *Illustrated Guide to the Scottish Economy* (London: Duckworth, 1999)

Radical Scotland (Edinburgh, 1987–1991)

Russell, Mike, *In Waiting* (Glasgow: Neil Wilson, 1999)

Saville, Richard, ed., *The Economic Development of Modern Scotland 1950–80* (Edinburgh: John Donald, 1985)

Scott, Sir Walter, *Rob Roy* (London: Dent, 1817)

Scottish Affairs, Edinburgh: Unit for the Study of Government in Scotland (1993–).

Smout, T. C., *A History of the Scottish People, 1560–1830* (Glasgow: Collins, 1969)

——, *A Century of the Scottish People, 1830–1950* (Glasgow: Collins, 1986)

Storrar, William, *Scottish Identity: A Christian Vision* (Edinburgh: Handsel, 1990)

Taylor, Alan, ed., *The Scottish Question* (London: Harper Collins, 2000)

Taylor, Brian, *The Scottish Parliament* (Edinburgh: Polygon at Edinburgh, 1999)

Walker, William M., *Juteopolis: Dundee and its Textile Workers, 1885–1923* (Edinburgh: Scottish Academic Press, 1979)

Wolfe, J. N., ed., *Government and Nationalism in Scotland* (Edinburgh: Edinburgh University Press, 1969)

Wright, Kenyon, *The People say Yes* (Colintraive: Argyll, 1998)

Yearbook of Scottish Government (Edinburgh: Polygon, 1974–93)

Index